Adrian Searle is a native of the Isle of Wight, from a long-established Island family. He was born in Ryde, where he currently lives, and has worked as a journalist and writer for more than thirty years. Passionate about the Island, and the maintenance of it's distinctive 'offshore' character, he has written extensively on the rich, colourful Wight heritage in newspapers, magazines and books. His previous work for the Dovecote Press, published in 1989, told the extraordinary story of the wartime years on the Isle of Wight between 1939 and 1945.

Following page
The 'Pepper Pot' – Britain's only surviving medieval lighthouse – stands defiant on St. Catherine's Hill above the notorious 'Bay of Death'.
(See St. Catherine's Pepper Pot)

ISLE OF WIGHT FOLKLORE

ADRIAN SEARLE

with illustrations by Dennis Burden

THE DOVECOTE PRESS

Dedicated to Lindsay – for so many reasons

First published in 1998 by the Dovecote Press Ltd
Stanbridge, Wimborne, Dorset BH21 4JD

ISBN 1 874336 63 3

© Adrian Searle 1998

Typeset in Sabon by The Typesetting Bureau
Wimborne, Dorset
Printed and bound by Baskerville Press, Salisbury, Wiltshire

1 3 5 7 9 8 6 4 2

CONTENTS

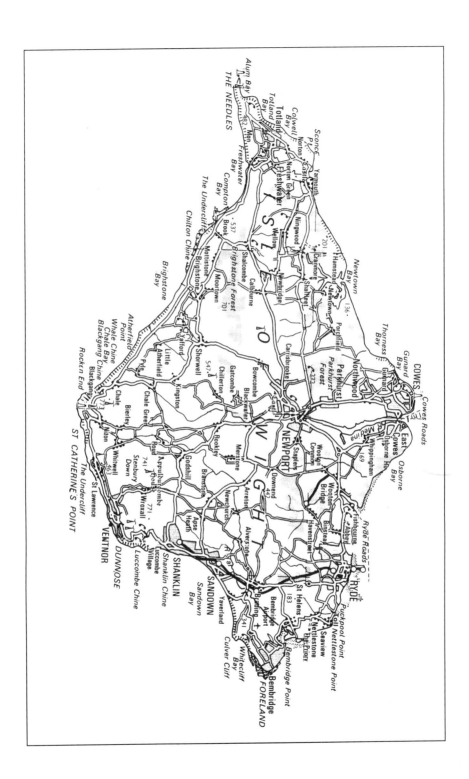

INTRODUCTION

The purpose of this book was to bring together the best of the Isle of Wight's colourful legends and folk tales with the traditions, customs and superstitions of its native people down the ages. Research revealed an abundance of material from which to choose. Like many offshore islands, Wight has a distinctive character of its own and this is fully reflected in an impressive catalogue of country lore.

The first decision, therefore, was what to leave out. Stories of ghosts and hauntings have been extensively covered by other writers – notably Gay Baldwin – in recent times. Thus, they have been largely omitted from this volume. For the same reason, the oft-recounted tales of smugglers and their illicit, but highly lucrative, Isle of Wight trade, have also been excluded. Many of the smuggling yarns were the invention of the smugglers themselves, scripted specifically to warn off the Customs men and anyone else tempted to venture into 'their' territory.

That still leaves a rich treasury of Island lore – stories linked to the origins of natural features, distinctive man-made structures, place-names, local characters, major events and ancient beliefs. Many of them are centuries old; several have undergone the 'Victorian treatment' – highly detailed narrative, often with an overt moral or religious message – at the hands of renowned local story-tellers such as Abraham Elder and Edward Turner. The degree of documented historical fact which forms the basis for most stories varies considerably. It is virtually non-existent in some cases; the charming legend of Godshill's founding is a perfect example. Conversely, a few of the stories – the arrest of the artist George Morland in the West Wight is a case in point – are accounts of events which can be largely, if not entirely, proven by historical record. These have passed into folklore because of the extraordinary circumstances surrounding them.

Some stories which fall into the 'extraordinary but true' category have been eliminated because so much has already been written about them, and it would be impossible to do them justice without devoting the whole of this book to their telling. The most obvious example is the story of Sophie Dawes' transition from the humblest of origins at St. Helens to fame and scandal as the 'Queen of Chantilly' in nineteenth century France.

Most of the customs and traditions described in these pages have, inevitably, died out (though there have been a few recent revivals). Factors in their demise include the advent of mass communication and easy travel; the dramatic decline in 'home grown' entertainment; the ever-increasing mechanisation of work on the land; and the general sophistication of twentieth century life. Some are still recalled by older Islanders; for the remainder, we are fortunate in being able to refer to the writings and guides to the local dialect of a few eminent scholars of Wight life, especially that master of the local tongue, W. H. Long. A number of locally-produced volumes on the history of the Island's more ancient towns – penned at a time when much of what was being written about was still within living memory – have further enlightened the search for the traditions of yesteryear.

The traditions and beliefs described are reflections of a vastly less complicated way of life; the dreamers among us may yearn for its return. Whether or not you take that view, the distinctive flavour of the Island's folklore has an absorbing fascination, and that, hopefully, should be sufficient to ensure its survival in the years to come.

As a footnote, it will be noted that the capital 'I' is used throughout the book to describe the Island. This is not a writer's whim; it is itself a long-established custom on Wight!

GOOD ST. BONIFACE

The celebrated Saxon martyr, St. Boniface, left his mark on the Isle of Wight. In fact, it's the highest mark there is on the Island – the towering down above Ventnor and Bonchurch which bears his name. Whether he actually set foot on it – indeed, on the Isle of Wight in general – is open to question. Yet there is a wealth of local tradition, a veritable stockpile of legend, which insists that he did cross the Solent.

Certain facts are known about St. Boniface, although the dates connected with them tend to vary in the written accounts of his life. He was born in the late seventh century, possibly in AD 680, and probably at Crediton in Devon. From there he travelled to join the Benedictine monastery at Nutscelle, near Winchester (at the age of thirteen, according to some accounts), where he was known to his fellow monks as Wynfryth. He became a priest around AD 710 and was eventually consecrated as a bishop by Pope Gregory II. Given the name of Boniface ('doer of good'), he was appointed Bishop of Mainz, carving his niche in history as the Apostle of Germany and laying the foundations for the Holy Roman Empire before his martyrdom in AD 755 at Dokkrum, near Leeuwarden, in what is now northern Holland.

Those are the basic facts. In all the many writings he left behind, St. Boniface provided not a shred of evidence to support the suggestion that he ever visited the Isle of Wight. Yet it remains a strong possibility, since he was within reasonable distance of the Island for a lengthy period prior to his departure for Germany. The legends abound. Some accounts suggest he made a series of missions from Nutscelle to the Island and preached to fishermen from what is today known as Pulpit Rock at Bonchurch. Others have him crossing the Solent during a sojourn in Southampton and suggest he 'laboured for some time' on the Island.

One day, we are told, a troubled Wynfryth (as he was still called) was walking along the shore near present-day Ventnor when he saw a boy dig a hole in the sand, fill a shell with sea water, then empty the water into the hole. The boy repeated the exercise for a while, then threw down the shell and burst into tears. On being asked the reason for his distress by Wynfryth, he explained: 'I wanted to empty the sea into the hole I dug, but I cannot do so.' To which Wynfryth responded: 'That is the cause of my own unhappiness. I have been trying to compass the infinite with my finite mind.' Apparently, Wynfryth had been plagued with religious doubts before his encounter with the boy. The episode clarified things for him and 'caused him to retire to his cell with his head at rest.'

A popular story which clearly links the saint with 'his' hill – though in its usual form, some time after his death – tells of a bishop who lost his way while riding the slopes of St. Boniface Down on a wild and stormy night. Dense mist or snow are optional variations. After a while his horse lost its footing and slid alarmingly down a precipice. The bishop let go of the reins, trusting to the horse's intuition and the spiritual guidance of St. Boniface, and vowing that, if he escaped with his life, he would donate an acre of land to the saint's church at Bonchurch, below the down. His trust was not misplaced – and Bishop's Acre survives to this day.

Some versions of the Bishop's Acre legend have the bishop's horse recovering its footing in the hollow of St. Boniface Well. Other accounts actually cast St. Boniface himself in the role of the lost horseman; still others simply describe the rider as 'a gentleman.' What many fail to point out is that Bishop's Acre is not actually in the village of Bonchurch but is today part of neighbouring Ventnor. However, if the legend has any foundation in fact – and historical records do not rule out the possibility – it must have been to the church at Bonchurch that the modest plot of land was dedicated. Ventnor 'grew out' of Bonchurch parish.

It may seem logical to assume that the dedication of Bonchurch's original Saxon church (if such a church there was) to St. Boniface is the origin for both the village's Domesday name of Bonecerce – cerc is the Anglo-Saxon for church – and its present title. However, another school of thought has it that the name is derived from Bana's church, or 'the church built by a murderer as an act of atonement.' The latter theory does not fit in at all with a version of one of the most enduring Isle of Wight legends, which suggests that monks from the Normandy abbey of Lyre founded the original church after landing on the adjacent shore in the eighth century. In its wildest form, the legend of Monks Bay goes further and credits the Normandy monks with the late introduction of Christianity to Wight – a feat more usually attributed to Bishop Wilfrid of York in the seventh century.

Much more plausible is the version of the legend which suggests that the monks came ashore at Bonchurch in the eleventh century to administer the affairs (notably the collection of tithes and rents in their parishes) of the six Island churches given to Lyre Abbey – a possession

The 'Old Church' of St. Boniface at Bonchurch. Was the church a
rebuilding by the Normans of a Saxon original?

of his – by the Lord of the Isle of Wight, William FitzOsbern. Bonchurch was not at that time a parish in its own right, but the legend suggests that the monks discovered the Saxon church there in a state of serious disrepair. As an act of thanksgiving for their safe arrival from France, they set about the job of repairing it for further use – and dedicated it to the martyred Saxon saint.

That might explain why the 'Old Church' at Bonchurch is a Norman structure – though a complete rebuild by the monks must have been required since the church contains absolutely nothing of Saxon origin. However, the seventeenth century diarist and historian Sir John Oglander attributed its construction to one Johannes de Argentine, a Frenchman, on land given to him by FitzOsbern.

The diminutive 'Old Church' was replaced in 1847-48 by the new church of St. Boniface, but was thankfully never demolished. After a period of total disuse, it is today again the setting for worship, but only on 5 June, St. Boniface Day, and Sunday evenings in June, July and August, when candlelit services are held. Nearby, the cove where the monks of Lyre are said to have come ashore is still known as Monks' Bay. Such are the fascinations of St. Boniface's legendary stamping ground.

THE HOLY WELLS

Improbably located at a site now virtually inaccessible near the summit of St. Boniface Down, the highest point on the Isle of Wight, is the most celebrated of the Island's 'holy wells'. These natural springs, revered for the supposed magical qualities of their waters, were often endowed with pagan legend before the arrival of Christianity saw their dedication by the Anglo-Saxons to one or other of the Christian martyrs.

In the case of St. Boniface Well, the present tense is used loosely. Although the well – dedicated, along with the hill on which it rises, to the martyred eighth century Saxon monk – does technically still exist, it is today little more than a damp patch of grass. Early nineteenth century guidebooks, produced in the days when the well was still providing a constant supply of water, tell us it was 'much venerated by the country people', who considered a spring at so great a height to be a natural phenomenon. The remarkable location of St. Bonny's Well, as it was known locally, gave rise to both legend and tradition:

> Louisa of the dark deep eyes, and Caroline of the raven locks, and Kate of the fair broad brow, oft-speeded – in all simplicity and with due faith – to the well of St. Boniface, and ere they drank of its lucent waters, silently formed the wishes on whose fulfilment their souls were most intent.

So ran the words of the old legend of St. Boniface Well. For its crystal clear water – described in 1856 as a 'limpid fountain' by the writer W. H. Davenport Adams – was said to possess a remarkable and useful property. This was a classic wishing well.

St. Boniface Down peaks at 787 feet above sea level, but the trek along the long, narrow path on its south face, trodden into rough steps by countless pairs of feet, was worth the effort once you had reached the fabled well some three-quarters of the way up – so long as you had managed to complete the climb without once looking back. If you had, you could take a drink from the spring water, in the comforting knowledge that any wish (up to three, according to some authorities) you chose to make whilst drinking was certain to be granted. Ships passing the supposedly holy site used to lower their topmasts as a mark of respect.

For many years it was customary for the young folk of Bonchurch village, beneath the down, to climb to the well on the saint's day in June and dress it with flowers – a custom also associated with 'holy wells' elsewhere. Only the occasional seeker-after-tradition now attempts to reach St. Bonny's Well. There's little in the way of directional guidance on the slopes of the down and, if you succeed in locating it, there's disappointingly little to see when you get there. St. Boniface's magic, like the spring water itself, seems to have dried up.

The site is nigh on impossible to reach today thanks to the twentieth century spread of holm oak on the slopes of the formerly treeless down, which has obliterated the old paths. A legend with more recent origins

St. Lawrence Well, showing the nineteenth century Gothic shrine
which houses the spring.

tells of a solitary man (some versions also describe a companion) who was in the habit of walking the down with his shooting stick and stopping every few feet to plant one of the vast quantity of acorns he had stuffed into his pockets before setting out. Some suggest that the mystery planter may have been Sir John Cheape, of Old Park, St. Lawrence, who laid great store on tree planting as a method of preventing, or at least arresting, the spread of soil erosion. The by-product was to transform the appearance of the great hill.

At St. Lawrence itself, and happily still very much in evidence, is the Gothic shrine enclosing the well dedicated – as is the diminutive twelfth century 'old' church nearby – to the third century martyr burnt to death on a gridiron during the Emperor Valerian's persecutions of the churchmen of Rome. When the first Earl of Yarborough added the present ornamentation early in the nineteenth century, St. Lawrence Well stood in a leafy dell by the side of the road from Ventnor. Diversion of this steep and narrow section of the old highway in 1864 divorced well from road; today, the old route serves as a footpath.

Shrine and spring are perfectly recognisable from a description given by Davenport Adams, writing not many years after Yarborough's work. It is 'surmounted with a cross, and encloses a bright spray-scattering stream which issues from a dolphin's mouth into a wide shell, and there ripples away beneath the road to mingle with the sea,' he wrote. Today, unlike the 'weary-footed Pilgrim of yore when he rested in the shadow of the Undercliff and slaked his thirst in the sweet well of St. Lawrence,' you are barred from sipping its cool waters. St. Lawrence Well must be worshipped – or at least admired – from the other side of a padlocked gate at the shrine entrance.

Also accorded 'holy well' status was the spring at nearby Niton which is the source of the Eastern Yar. Dr. John Whitehead, who wrote extensively of Niton and the adjacent Undercliff in the early years of the present century, suggests that it was known as such until fairly recent times. Follow the Eastern Yar north-eastwards and you reach the Island's other celebrated 'holy well' in a mysterious copse near Brading – and legendary St. Urian's Well merits a story all of its own.

THE LOST CITY OF WOLVERTON

On the slopes of the high ground to the east of Brading lies the most mysterious woodland of Wight. Centurion's Copse is the haunt of historical fact and legend, interwoven through the centuries into a rich tapestry of enduring fascination. How much of what has been written about the place is actually fact remains a matter for delightful conjecture.

That there was something here before ash, hazel and oak combined to form a dense protective canopy is beyond question. The first clues to former importance are the cobblestones on the footpath sloping westwards, down to the copse, from the Bembridge-Yarbridge road, at a right-angled turn before Longlands Farm. Then there is the tantalising reference to 'earthworks' alongside the copse on the Ordnance Survey maps. The earthworks in question were discovered during a partial excavation of the site in the nineteenth century and are almost certainly those of the mediaeval manor house of Wolverton (written as Wolverton-in-Brading to distinguish it from Wolverton Manor at Shorwell). The footpath to the present-day Centurion's Copse was once the cobbled drive to the manor house, which survived at least until the sixteenth century reign of Edward VI.

That much is fact, as is the former existence nearby of a small chapel dedicated to the eighth century Breton prelate St. Urian. A few stones from the chapel were still to be found at the turn of the present century, according to Victorian guidebooks. Until the existence of St. Urian was conclusively proven at about the same time by the Rev. E. Boucher James in his *Letters Relating to the Isle of Wight*, it was commonly believed that the name of the saint (together with the chapel and copse which bore it) was a corruption of the word 'centurion.' It was a reasonable assumption considering the proximity of Roman relics, culminating with the discovery in 1879 of Brading's Roman Villa at Morton. The corruption, however, was the other way round. It was St. Urian's name that was rolled into centurion, and Sir John Oglander's diaries reveal that the corrupted form was in use at least as far back as the mid-sixteenth century.

But why was St. Urian's chapel built in the first place? At this point historical fact and mysterious legend begin to merge. According to some stories, Centurion's Copse was once the location not merely of a mediaeval manor, but of the 'lost city' of Wolverton, which thrived on the banks of Brading Haven many centuries before the reclamation of that great expanse of water from the sea. While it is quite conceivable that a settlement of some sort did exist on the site, the substitution of 'village' for 'city' would probably be nearer the historical mark.

Whatever the status of Wolverton, it would not have been surprising had the fame of St. Urian reached the settlement, and prompted the dedication of its chapel in his name, at a time when foreign monastic establishments were common on the Island. That being the case, it is easy to accept that the people of Wolverton, finding a natural spring in their midst with supposedly magical properties, should similarly dedicate this 'holy well' to St. Urian – and it is around St. Urian's Well that the colourful legend of Wolverton's dramatic demise is woven.

The legend is set in the early part of the fourteenth century. Wolverton was regularly visited by an old man, shabbily dressed, who not only sold small trinkets to the people, but also dispensed sound advice about their personal problems, and was thus highly regarded. His daily chores at an end, he would leave Wolverton and take the pathway towards the coast at Culver Cliff, where it was assumed he lived in a cave – though nobody ever summoned up the nerve to follow him there. However, despite the Hermit of Culver's good influence on Wolverton, some of its people suddenly began to suffer all manner of ill fortune.

The Hermit told them it was all the fault of 'a stranger, dressed in a grey cowl', who would shortly be paying Wolverton a visit with the most sinister of motives – to poison the waters of the revered well. This was the worst possible news. The people knew from the Hermit's own prophesy (or from an engraved verse on a stone column by the well – depending on which version of the legend you rely) that Wolverton would thrive only so long as St. Urian's Well remained untainted. Disaster would befall the place if the purity of the water was marred, and the Ness, the great bulwark of Culver, would crash into the sea.

Before long, a figure whose appearance was exactly as described by the Hermit of Culver, arrived at the well. The words he uttered as he leaned over the brink (to lay a palm frond in the water, according to some sources) made no sense to those who watched him, some of whom were certain he was about to poison the water. The stranger was pelted with stones until he lay dead on the ground, his blood spilling into the spring. Too late did the people of Wolverton discover that the man whose blood now tainted the pure waters of St. Urian's Well was an innocent pilgrim from the Holy Land come to worship

Legend has it that Yaverland's Church of St. John the Baptist was moved
on rollers to its current site from the 'lost city' of Wolverton in
what is now Centurion's Copse.

at the spring. They were to pay the heaviest of penalties for their
misjudgment.

True to the prophesy, Culver's Ness fell with a thunderous roar, and
Wolverton was burnt to the ground, never to be rebuilt. Legend and
fact mingle again for it is suggested that the burning of the 'city' took
place at the hands of the French, whose landing at nearby St. Helens in
1340 is a well-documented historical fact. The same cannot be said
for the tradition that St. Urian's Chapel was moved on rollers –
presumably after the fall of Wolverton – to form the church at nearby
Yaverland. Today, Centurion's Copse is said to be haunted by the
tragic pilgrim, face hidden by the grey cowl. You may see him if
you visit the garlic-strewn wood. You will almost certainly notice
the strange indefinable atmosphere, and wonder at the almost total
absence of bird song. A truly mysterious place.

THE HERMIT OF CULVER

Who was the Hermit of Culver? Was he a force for good? Or for evil? Some versions of Wolverton's legend remove any doubts on that score – particularly a trilogy of tales which concludes with the story of 'Daring Tom', the only inhabitant of the doomed city ever to enter the hermit's extraordinary home at Culver. In this three-part account, embroidered (if not actually invented) by imaginative Victorian story-tellers, the hermit becomes the sinister 'Mysterious Merchant'.

His visits to Wolverton – first on a monthly basis, then more frequently, and always late in the afternoon – are recounted as before. The goods he brings to sell are tempting, his prices low, and his manners impeccable. The merchant is more than welcome and his apparent ability to tell the fortunes of the local folk increases his popularity still further. He possesses, too, an uncanny gift for judging, by their countenance alone, those among the resident population who are in debt. To these people he offers loans, producing gold coins to ease their worries and, oddly, indicating not the slightest interest in ever retrieving his money.

However, as each of the debtors approached by him are to find out, repayment is expected in kind.

'My good friend, I don't want the money,' he tells them, 'but I have a spite against so-and-so. He has been running me down. If you will set fire to his rick we will call it quits!'

The debtor's fear of detection is calmed by the merchant's assurance that 'no-one who follows my direction will ever be found out.' Thus, the true, evil nature of the Mysterious Merchant becomes known to the people of Wolverton. They still depend on him, but now they also greatly fear and detest him.

He offers help in all manner of situations, but always a favour is demanded in return – and the favour usually entails setting fire to someone's property. Increasingly, the merchant's visits bring havoc in the city. It is noted by the people that he is particularly active before 'any great mischief' takes place. This is certainly the case immediately before the tragedy at St. Urian's Well – the common link between all versions of the Wolverton legend – which precipitates the destruction of the city. The merchant is frequently in town, winning back the affections of the people by giving remedies for the sick, writing letters for the illiterate and carrying out general acts of kindness without reward. Yet, he tells them, his good works are threatened 'by a man who is hiding in the neighbourhood.'

Then come the familiar elements of the legend: the description of the supposed villain with his grey cowl, the warning of the threat he poses to the purity of the spring water, the prophesy of the city's downfall, the attack on the innocent holy man, and the fall of Wolverton. This version, however, suggests the merchant is the cause of the disaster – and the final part of the trilogy exposes him for what he really is. It is set in the period between the tragedy at the well and the city's fall.

We are told how Daring Tom shares his fellow citizens' curiosity as to the whereabouts and precise nature of the merchant's home. All any of them know is that the mysterious visitor always makes for the high downs and cliffs at Culver when his day's work is done and then seems to disappear into the ground. (Another version of the legend has the merchant apparently turning into a thorn bush if, for just a moment,

Culver Cliff, with the monument to the 1st Earl of Yarborough just visible on Culver Down.

the curious Wolverton people take their eyes off him.) Young Tom determines to solve the mystery and, soon after the death of the holy man, he seizes his opportunity. The merchant is back in town – for his first visit since the tragedy – and from his manner no-one would guess anything untoward has happened in the city. He seems to have no knowledge of the curse which 'like a pall' now rests over the place. Few, however, will talk with him.

Fortified by liberal quantities of ale, Daring Tom follows the merchant as he leaves Wolverton that evening. He plucks up the courage to ask him where he lives. The old man invites him to 'come and see' and leads the hero of the tale to the very edge of Culver Cliff. An opening appears in the ground and Tom is led inside. He enters a 'brilliantly-lighted hall, the most conspicuous picture in it being a large portrait of the merchant himself.' Around the hall are also hung 'striking likenesses' of many of the people of Wolverton. Curiously, each has a black mark on their forehead. Tom notices an unfinished painting and suspects he may be the intended subject.

He is, however, entertained 'in grand style and on a lavish scale by a number of mysterious beings' in the merchant's home. Music and dancing while away the hours. Tom feels he is 'in an uncanny place,' and wonders if he will be able to escape 'from the weird abode in the bowels of the earth.' But he braves it out and, when his escape comes, it is dramatic. Supper is laid – 'a very tempting fast' – and Tom is about to begin when he remembers that no grace has been said. He bows his head and repeats the words taught him by a good friar in Wolverton. As he begins, the lights go out and when he mentions the name of God 'the whole company shrieks with terror.' Thunderous crashes follow, the roof collapses and Tom fears for his life. Then, miraculously, he is found lying 'in a dazed condition' at the top of the cliff the next morning. 'Daring Tom was confident that he had narrowly escaped detention by Satan himself,' we are told in Edward Turner's turn-of-the-century account. Tom will boast that he has saved Wolverton from any further attention by the Mysterious Merchant – with some justification since this sinister character is never again seen in the city. Then again, nor is anyone else – once the curse of the tainted spring waters has taken its toll.

It's a good story, and one worth remembering if you seek out the remains of the merchant's distinctive home today. It's still there, a little below the brink of the cliffs, but tradition prefers the option that this was the abode of a man of God, rather than the Devil. The cavern has for centuries been known as the Hermit's Hole.

THE LEGENDARY
WOODLANDS

Centurion's Copse is one of several Island woodlands with legendary associations. Particularly colourful local traditions also surround the naming of Trooper's Wood, near Shorwell; Money Coppice, part of Barton Wood at East Cowes; the wooded knoll of Queen's Bower, not far from Alverstone; and especially Elenor's Grove, at Quarr, which boasts a truly remarkable Isle of Wight legend.

Elenor's Grove is familiar to motorists as a section of the main road from Ryde to Newport, but the road takes its name from the small wood which abuts it to the south, opposite the driveway to Quarr Abbey, and the wood is named, but misspelt, after Eleanor of Aquitaine, Henry II's rebellious queen. The legend suggests that Eleanor, during the long period of imprisonment imposed on her by Henry from 1173, was incarcerated at the original Cistercian abbey of Quarr. This does not conflict over much with the broad brush of historical fact, since Eleanor's movements during this period were indeed confined to the south of England, though her travelling was usually restricted to the short distances between Winchester, Salisbury, Ludgershall and other royal residences on the mainland.

If the legend is to be believed, while at Quarr she developed a fondness for wandering in its sequestered glades. So enchanted was Eleanor that she directed her grave should be made 'beneath the shade of the melancholy boughs.' In the event, Eleanor of Aquitaine was interred alongside Henry in the abbey of Fontevrault, the Plantagenets' burial church in France – where the tomb can still be seen – so the last bit of the legend, which insists that she was buried instead in a golden coffin at Quarr, is pure fantasy. Unless, that is, you believe in magic!

Her coffin is said to have had a magic spell placed upon it, and is supposed to lie beneath those 'melancholy boughs' where we are told Eleanor once walked, concealed beneath a golden door at the end of an underground passage. Whatever the truth of the old legend, the little woodland has for centuries been known as Queen Eleanor's Grove. While, in modern times, the name has been abbreviated and corrupted, it remains in common usage ... a fact no doubt to the liking of Eleanor's ghost, which reputedly haunts the site to this day.

Remnants of the original Quarr Abbey, converted into a house and farm buildings and still recognisable today more than a century after this drawing was commissioned by Percy Stone for his *Architectural Antiquities of the Isle of Wight* in 1891. Were these buildings and the nearby woodlands known to Eleanor of Aquitaine?

The legends connected with Trooper's Wood and Money Coppice both have their origins in the English Civil War – but are very different in character. Trooper's Wood is the site of an old withy bed behind the Elizabethan manor house of Wolverton, south-west of Shorwell village. It takes its name from a Civil War trooper who supposedly sank to his death in the treacherous wetland, and whose heavy footsteps are said to have haunted the area for centuries afterwards.

Money Coppice popularly owes its name to Eustace Mann, owner of the Osborne estate at the time of the Civil War's outbreak. Fearful of the confiscation of his land and possessions under a Parliamentary commonwealth, Mann took the precaution of at least preserving his fortune in gold and silver coins by burying them in Barton Wood! According to the story, this proved a highly successful hiding-place. No-one discovered Eustace Mann's money. Not even Eustace! With the monarchy safely restored, he returned to the wood to recover his buried treasure. However, he had neglected to mark the spot and couldn't remember where the coins lay hidden. Frantic searching proved fruitless.

If the story is true – and it is perhaps one of the more plausible Isle of Wight legends – then presumably Eustace Mann's money still lies buried in Barton Wood. The area of woodland which reputedly holds the treasure has long been known as Money Coppice. While the link between the name and Mann's lost fortune is irresistible, there may be a rather more prosaic origin – since the ground in Barton Wood has in the past yielded a hoard of coins from the first and second centuries.

It was Eustace Mann's grand-daughter who married into the Blatchford family, from whose descendant, Lady Isabella Blatchford, the original Osborne House and its estate were purchased by Queen Victoria in 1845 for redevelopment as a sumptuous royal palace. But which monarch did the people responsible for naming a wooded knoll in the once extensive forest of Borthwood have in mind when they called it Queen's Bower? We can be certain it wasn't Victoria.

The origin of Queen's Bower is tied to an earlier era – but which particular era is open to question. Most agree that this was the site of a hunting-lodge in the days when Borthwood was well stocked with a variety of game. It may be that the bower in question was named in honour of Queen Anne, who some suggest visited the woodland for its excellent hawking during her reign in the early years of the eighteenth century. Alternatively, the high royal status of Phillipa, Duchess of York, to whom the copse was granted by Henry V in 1415, may have provided the inspiration. Or was the 'queen' in question a monarch in strictly Isle of Wight terms . . . the truly remarkable Isabella de Fortibus, Lady of the Wight, and the last private owner of the Island? Tradition has it that the hunting-lodge was indeed built for Isabella, whose energetic 'reign' as effective monarch ended with her death in 1293.

LEGENDS OF THE
BLOODSTONES

There is a curious connection between a spring rising at the foot of a quiet copse to the north-west of Brading and the natural gorge turned coastal theme park at tourist-saturated Blackgang Chine. Some 13 miles apart, the two locations are linked by the legends of the bloodstones – two markedly different stories with a common theme.

The stones in question are the red-spotted pebbles and flints which can sometimes be found lying in the bed of a stream. Their appearance is scientifically explained as the result of red algae clinging *en masse* to the top of the stones – one of several plausible reasons offered for the reddish appearance of springs and streams in many areas of the British Isles. However, the effect this can give when the pebbles are viewed from above the water is one of a trail of blood. Not surprisingly, it has given rise to a number of – literally – colourful traditions.

Bloodstone Well was the apt name given to the spring near Brading, rising on the old manorial boundary between Nunwell and Ashey in what is now known as Bloodstone Copse. Scientific logic is one thing; at Bloodstone Well, the traditional explanation for the 'large spots of blood' on the bed of the spring owed nothing whatsoever to science and everything to superstition and folklore. For it was said that the red colouring was the blood of Saxons and Danes who fought a fearsome battle in the vicinity of the well. The legendary origin for the name of the copse and its well is now a feature (along with the scientific explanation) of information panels erected recently by Hampshire and Isle of Wight Wildlife Trust at the footpath entrances to Bloodstone and neighbouring Eaglehead Copse. And, in certain light, the spring water does indeed have a reddish hue.

That the marauding Danes fought the Saxons on the Isle of Wight is a well-established historical truth. In fact, the *Anglo-Saxon Chronicle* suggests there may have been several bloody encounters between them in the 120 years or so which followed the first visit to Wight by the Viking raiders in 897. They 'did much harm' that year in a battle which is believed – though not universally agreed – to have been fought in the waters of Brading Haven. Very close indeed to the spring at Bloodstone.

The 'battle' legend seems more or less specific to Bloodstone, but

Thomas Barber's engraving of Blackgang Chine was originally produced
for his classic *Picturesque Illustrations* early in the nineteenth
century and dramatically depicts the abrupt fall of the legendary
'bloodstained rill' into the sea.

is on a par with the many other traditions which have sprung up as
explanation for the reddish appearance of flowing water. More common
are the tales which link 'red wells' to the murder of a revered personage
or, conversely, to the destruction of a noted local tyrant. Into the latter
category falls the enduring legend of the Giant of Chale – the oldest tale
of Blackgang.

Truly monstrous in his habits and lifestyle, this most fearsome Isle of
Wight giant . . .

> . . . was mighty and big,
> And he loved man's flesh better than pig.
> And steamed the fat ones in their own gravy.
> The children he bound with bands of wire,
> And roasted them alive on a charcoal fire.

The ogre lived in a cave at Blackgang at some indeterminate period of
history, his darkly sinister home contrasting horribly with the colour
and beauty of the chine. According to the legend, a holy man –

he is sometimes called a saint – determined to put an end to the giant's decidedly unholy activities. Although old and understandably frightened of the ogre, the hero of the tale ventured forth to Blackgang, armed only with a staff of mountain ash. The sight that met his eyes on arrival at the cave was gruesome. The ogre's home was paved with the bones of dead men, and the giant himself sat on a throne of human skulls, surrounded by scorpions, adders, toads and 'dragons with scaly wings'. Horrified, the holy man could neither speak nor pray.

He did, however, manage to make the sign of the cross – and with this his courage returned. Now he cursed both the giant and the ground which had been the monster's home:

> Nor flowers nor fruit this earth shall bear;
> But all shall be dark, and waste, and bare!
> Nor shall the ground give footing dry
> To beasts that walk, or birds that fly;
> But a poisonous stream shall run to the sea,
> Bitter to taste, and bloody to see!
> And the earth it shall crumble and crumble away
> And crumble on till the Judgment Day.

As the holy man spoke, he was enveloped by a swirling mist. When it finally cleared, the cave in which he had been standing had disappeared – and the Giant of Chale with it. Nor was there any colour left in the once beautiful landscape . . . only a bloodstained rill flowing among the black earth and rocks of Blackgang Chine.

And the dark, lifeless earth at Blackgang has, indeed, crumbled and crumbled away. So much so that the famous chine, and the red-pebbled stream which once flowed through it down to the sea – providing a far from dry 'footing' for the smugglers who frequented this route in abundance – now ends half-way up the cliff face, forcing a progressive inland retreat for the theme park and its multitude of attractions. Victims of relentless coastal erosion . . . or a holy man's curse.

SHRINKAGE AND SACRIFICE

Two of the other high downs which with St. Boniface form the southern bulwark of the Isle of Wight are also associated with curious – though quite different – local traditions. The first is a simple and straightforward anecdotal reference to a natural phenomenon which is itself anything but simple and straightforward. The second, bound up as it is with the pagan rituals of ancient Wight, is a considerably more complex story to relate. Yet, unlike the first tradition, its meaning is perfectly clear – the triumph of Christian values over the old logic and beliefs.

Logic and belief are generally suspended when it comes to recounting the tradition of Week Down, which rises in what eighteenth century writers loosely described as 'the intermediate way' between St. Catherine's Point and Shanklin Down. Not only rises – but falls, it would seem! Sir Richard Worsley, writing in 1781, told of Chale men recalling an inexplicable development in the local geography which had occurred since their youth. As young men they could barely see Shanklin Down above Week Down when looking from Chale (later St. Catherine's) Down. Not only that, but older villagers had told them there was a time when it could only be seen from the top of the signal beacon on Chale Down.

Yet, during their lifetime, Shanklin Down had become clearly visible from Chale Down. So, either it had risen in height or Week Down had considerably sunk! The anecdote was subsequently repeated by other writers, none of whom attempted to offer a rational explanation for this extraordinary occurrence. 'So wonderful are the operations of nature that it is not for me to say "It cannot be" but this is an event so far out of her usual course that I own I could not readily give credit to it,' wrote the artist Hassell in his account of a late-eighteenth century tour of the Island.

Week Down seems to have stayed put over the last couple of hundred years, its apparent eighteenth century movement dismissed as the stuff of legend by modern scientists and geologists. What would the pre-Christian pagans have made of it centuries before? They would not have scoffed. Possibly, fearing the gods had been offended, they would have offered a sacrifice. Innocent little children, perhaps.

On nearby Wroxall Down, according to legend, three 'innocent little children' were once the focus of sombre attention as the people of the southern part of the Island gathered on the hilltop in the days before the Wight's late conversion to Christianity. The general appearance of the people, we are told, was 'rough and savage.' Approaching a group of them, 'an unknown man, of pleasant countenance' asked the meaning of the crowd. 'It is the day of the giving of the children,' said one. 'Our enemies have conquered us; our cattle have died; our food is scanty, the gods are angry. We will give to them the children, and they will prosper us again.'

In this Victorian account of the legend of Wroxall Down, the stranger is henceforth referred to as the 'Unknown One'. He tells the savage Islanders they are making a mistake. The slaughter of innocent children will bring nothing to them but sorrow. 'Why had these three children been taken from their homes to be killed? Was it not because their parents had nothing to offer that their lives might be spared? Had not others, by bribing the captors, saved their own children?' Predictably for a folk tale catering for a Victorian readership, 'the people feel the truth of the words and began to doubt the efficacy of their offering.'

The Unknown One then passes from group to group and is listened to 'with attention.' But, in the meantime, the preparation for the sacrifice is going ahead. The little victims – 'pretty children, two girls and a boy of tender years' – are decorated with flowers, but their hands are tied. Possibly, they do not realise the part they are to play in the tragedy. At the sight of a 'rough looking man, armed with a murderous knife,' one child begins to cry and the other two join in out of sympathy. 'Was there no answering throb in the heart of the multitude?' asks the author (in this case, Edward Turner). There wasn't – but the hero of the tale is about to take matters in hand. Just at the moment of highest tension and expectancy, the Unknown One is seen standing between the children and the executioner.

'Beware!' he says, 'touch not one of those little ones, for their Heavenly Father will not hold you guiltless if you harm his children.' Before the leaders can recover from their surprise, the 'fearless visitor' has picked up the children and passed them to 'friendly hands,' thus removing them from immediate danger. But, of course, the leaders are furious. 'They rushed upon the Unknown One with fierce cries. He resisted not. He was satisfied that he had saved the children.' In their anger, the men of violence throw him from the head of the down and then (as if that wasn't enough) proceed to 'beat the life out of him with heavy stones.'

However, the dramatic legend concludes, 'from that time forward, never more was the life of a child offered as a sacrifice in the Isle of

Wight. The spirit of the Unknown One was said to hover over the place where he fell, and the children for many a day came with flowers to testify their love for the Wroxall martyr.'

It is perfectly possible – if not probable – that this story is based on fact. Pagan beliefs and rituals survived longer in the Isle of Wight, which traditionally (according to no less an authority than the Venerable Bede) was 'the last of all the British provinces . . . to accept the faith of Christ.' Whether Wroxall Down really did play such a significant role in the banishment of the old religious practices is a matter for conjecture. It was not the spirit of the Unknown One hovering over the place, but rather the buzzards (or *wroc*), which gave the village its name.

THE FLOODING OF
BRADING HAVEN

Most enduring of the folklore tales which recall Druidical influence on the Isle of Wight is the tradition linking the Druids to the original flooding of Brading Haven. This is particularly so with the written accounts penned before the Haven's reclamation from the sea in the 1870s, when it was perhaps felt expedient to submerge the evidence of pre-Christian faith and ritual beneath the waves.

Interestingly, the legend of Brading Haven has as its central feature an historical fact. During Sir Hugh Myddleton's temporarily successful attempt to reclaim 700 acres of the flooded Haven in the seventeenth century, a stone-encased well was discovered near its centre – proof positive that water had been sought from the ground before it became an all-prevailing feature above it. Country lore (enhanced by fanciful nineteenth century writers) has it that this was a sacred well of the Druids, out of which the waters of the mighty Haven were eventually to gush forth.

The 'Hexel ground' of the River Yar – location of the eventual Haven – has been identified as the most revered of all Druidical sites in the land of Guitt, as the ancient Britons styled the Island (ranking above the original Needle rock and the Longstone at the site of a Neolithic barrow on Mottistone Down). Here stood a sacred grove of oaks, among which the stone-encased well had been sunk. Once a year at this place, a living man, bound within a wicker-work cage above a pile of wood, was ceremonially sacrificed to the gods as a burnt offering. This much, more or less, is common to all surviving written accounts of Brading Haven's extraordinary legend.

In its simpler form – favoured by Abraham Elder in his classic *Tales and Legends* of 1839 – the story relates how the sacrificial proceedings were interrupted one year by a violent thunder storm. 'The well burst forth and, with a mighty roar, the sea broke in and swept away almost everything,' wrote Elder. This somewhat basic version is enlivened by the writer's detailed references to the 'enormous stature' of some of the assembled Druids – notably Coll, the Archdruid, 'being over seven cubits in height.' A cubit was approximately the length of a forearm.

A later re-telling of the story casts three 'baptised strangers' in a leading role. They arrive on the Isle of Wight, 'poorly dressed, and not come to hunt, nor to fight, nor to engage in trade,' according to Edward Turner's fanciful account, which describes how the three gladly share the hospitality offered by the native people. Inevitably, the strangers are 'very learned and wise'. They tell of the sacrifice of Christ – and the message is well received by many of the people. Not so the Druids. Fearing a loss of influence, they regard the strangers with suspicion.

Eventually, the setting of Turner's story moves to the Haven. He tells of the Druids walking to the grove to cut mistletoe from the oaks and, as was their custom, 'testing the knowledge' of the strangers who accompanied them. Various rites and ceremonies are gone through, water is drawn from the sacred well and the Druids gather round the pile to prepare for the annual offering of human flesh.

It is time for the anonymous strangers to do their bit. 'Ancient Druids,' proclaims one, 'you know the prophecy that was spoken, that the perfect sacrifice was the blood of one man that had a woman for his mother, and had no man for his father.'

'Find us such a one, and we will sacrifice him,' the Archdruid responds.

The narrative continues in similar vein. The Druids are accused of 'sacrificing to the evil spirits of the deep' and of 'corrupting the worship' of the people. In angry retaliation, they protest that the strangers are 'betraying our mystery' and demand 'a treble expiation.' Whereupon, the trio are seized, bound and placed in the wicker cage on top of the pile. Torches set the dry brushwood alight.

'The red fire is mounting. Vengeance is reaching them,' the Archdruid cries out – but his words are interrupted. Lightning flashes into his eyes, blinding him, and thunder rolls.

The storm ceases. For a moment there is silence, broken only by the crackling fire. Then there is 'a mighty sound of rushing water, like a swollen winter's torrent pouring from the hills with unstoppable power,' Turner's tale continues. The water rises from the holy well, fifty feet into the air, and then descends, spreading its deluge. It is followed by 'a terrible roaring, like all the storms of the winter rolled into one,' as the sea rushes over everything in one mighty wave.

Only the three strangers survive. The wicker basket which had so recently incarcerated them now carries them safely to their freedom on dry land. 'But,' writes Turner, 'the sea returned not to the deep, and the Hexel ground of Yar lies beneath the water. The oaks no longer swing their branches to the breeze, but the waves roll over the spot. Yet, the message brought by the strangers was not forgotten.'

Other versions of the legend suggest the Haven was flooded as the

An early nineteenth century engraving of Brading and the yet-to-be reclaimed expanse of the Haven which, according to legend, had centuries before 'burst forth' from the Druid's Well.

result of a doomed attempt to draw from the well, by means of sorcery, a forbidden treasure concealed within it – or through the releasing of a water spirit trapped inside. The Brading Haven legend has also appeared in verse. W. H. Davenport Adams chose a 'rudely rhymed' technique to tell the story in his 1856 history of Wight, though his version of the tale flooded the haven in Norman times when an ancient prophesy – 'woe unto him who uncovers this well!' – was mocked with dramatic consequences. Davenport Adams' six verses conclude:

> And never again shall the dark oaks be
> Where Ocean laughs in triumphant glee!
> Then ever the truth of the proverb we'll own -
> ' 'Tis prudent to let the well alone!'

Sir Hugh Myddleton may well have agreed with that. Just ten years after his workmen uncovered the well in their attempt to permanently drain the land in 1620, the sea burst in again. Jabez Balfour finally succeeded in holding back the water with his – so far – permanent reclamation of Brading Haven in 1878. Yet Balfour, too, was cursed. The reclamation was rocked by scandal. He ended up in Parkhurst!

THE LEGEND OF GODSHILL

Those who delve into the origins of Isle of Wight place-names are not much troubled by Godshill. 'Self-explanatory' is the note usually appended. This is perfectly true. The name of the Island's most noted picture-postcard village is simply derived from God's Hill. But that's where self-explanation ends . . . and legend begins.

All Saints Church at Godshill, easily the most photographed of all the Island's churches, occupies a strikingly commanding position above a cluster of pretty-as-a-picture cottages and gardens which have long proved irresistible. The spacious church dates from the fourteenth century and is probably the fourth to have existed on the site. Godshill was one of the six Isle of Wight churches gifted to the Normandy abbey of Lyre by its founder, William FitzOsbern, Lord of the Isle of Wight, in the eleventh century.

The legend tells the story of the founding of the first Godshill church, and is generally set – but this tends to vary – round about the time of the Island's late conversion to Christianity in the seventh century. Whatever the precise timing, we are told that the site of the present-day village was inhabited by people whose lives were still governed by the old pagan beliefs and traditions. One day, a holy man arrived among them to begin the task of Christian conversion.

His mission met with spectacular success. Casting aside the blood-stained altars in favour of the 'new' religion, the village elders declared: 'We will build a Temple unto the Lord, and we will worship him there; we and all our children, and our children's children, and ages yet unborn shall know how the Saxon reverenced God.' The location for the church was chosen, the foundations were marked out, and huge stones were piled one upon the other – all in the space of a single day. At nightfall, no doubt exhausted by this mighty endeavour, the villagers stopped work for a well-earned rest. They awoke to an astonishing sight.

The location they had chosen for their church was at the foot of a hill. Overnight, the stones painstakingly manoeuvred into position the day before, had been removed and transported, by some unseen force, to the very top of the hill. Mystified, but undeterred, the builders tried again to put up their church on the site they had determined for it. Again, as they slept, the stones were whisked away to the hilltop. This

According to the charming legend of Godshill, the hilltop was the preferred
location for the village church: but did it move itself?

apparently happened several times more before the message sank in.
'Let us build unto the Creator a Temple on the summit of the hill,' the
village elders proclaimed, 'for of a truth it will be acceptable to him; and
from this time forth shall the sanctuary and the village be known unto
men, in remembrance of this great deed, as God's Hill!' And so it was.

As with most legends, there are variations to Godshill's story. One
has the 'holy man' – sometimes he is referred to as a Bishop –
supervising the building work. We are told that, after the mysterious
movement of the stones on the first night, he posted two guards to watch
over the foundations once they had been returned to base. At midnight
on the second evening the watchmen heard rumblings from the
foundations, then watched in amazement as the stones began to move,
rolling and scrambling up the hill. The smaller stones hopped and
skipped over the obstacles they encountered; the larger ones apparently
groaned with the exertion!

With the stones went marker pegs. At the summit, stones and pegs –
the latter knocked into place by a spade, wielded by an unseen hand –
carefully arranged themselves, as they had the night before, in position
for building work to commence. Clearly, it was agreed, a miraculous
agent was at work. The ground at the summit was consecrated by the
holy man, and construction work on the hilltop church began.

Connected with this version is the suggestion that the land originally
earmarked for the church at the foot of the hill was owned by a farmer

with few, if any, religious convictions. He strongly objected to the building of a place of Christian worship on his land, craftily arguing that he was unworthy of such an honour because of his many sins! The holy man got round that problem by immediately granting absolution to the farmer – who was nevertheless suspected of being somehow responsible for the movement of the stones when it first occurred. Maybe he was working to the instructions of Satan himself. That was the belief of those people who decided to call the land 'rejected' by the stones the Devil's Acre.

Even more fanciful is the version of the legend which attributes the movement of the stones to the fairies, who 'toiled unceasingly to transport them to the hilltop' because the originally-chosen site was the place in which they held their revels! The Godshill legend, in one or other of its many forms, has been around for centuries, adding considerable mystique to the 'self-explanatory' origin of the village name.

NEWTOWN'S PIED PIPER

Closely resembling the story of the Pied Piper of Hamelin, immortalised by Robert Browning, the Isle of Wight's own legend of the musical rat-catcher's revenge takes us back to the fourteenth century, to the days when Francheville, the former identity of tranquil Newtown, was a flourishing town and sea port. It was, however, a town with a problem.

Rats had overrun the place, nibbling their way into granaries, rooms and cupboards. Scarcely any food could be saved from them. They even drank the stocks of wine, mead and beer, gnawing a hole in the top of the cask, drinking as far as their noses could reach, and then dipping their tails in for the other rats to suck. The town's infants were watched night and day to prevent the rats from eating their noses and nibbling their fingers. Despite the constant vigil, many children were maimed by the rats before they were strong enough to defend themselves.

Cats were introduced, happily helping themselves to the abundant source of nourishment. Then the rats developed a taste for kittens – and the cat population dwindled. So the town's burgesses tried poison. Many rats were destroyed, but the stench of their rotting bodies pervaded the streets and houses; eventually, an infectious disease developed and a great number of people died. Rewards tempted the rat-catchers, but their efforts all ended in disappointment. And then came the Piper.

Fantastically dressed in a multi-coloured costume, he sought out the Mayor and asked what reward he would receive for ridding the town of its scourge. The Mayor called the burgesses together for an agonising debate in which the merits of much-loved economy were weighed against the desperate need to rid the town of its rats. The latter argument won the day, for the Piper was told he would be paid the equivalent of £500 – an enormous sum for the time – when all the rats were extinct. He left the Town Hall playing a merry tune on his pipe.

As the Piper marched on through the streets of Francheville, the rats appeared from all directions and began to trot along behind him. Every 50 yards or so he would stop, turn around and play a particular flourish on his pipe to allow time for the young toddling rats to catch up. Up Silver Street he went, down Gold Street, then on to the harbour. Fascinated, the people followed as the Piper led the, by now, seething mass of rats to the water's edge. He climbed into a high-sided boat, too

The Town Hall, Newtown. The Town Hall was built in 1677, exactly three centuries after the devastating French raid on what was once an important medieval port, and the legendary location for the Island's version of the cautionary tale of the Pied Piper.

high for the rats to do the same, and punted himself into the deeper water. Mesmerised by his merry music, and wagging their tails, the rats followed the boat. The Piper played on, the rats paddling around him, until the tide had fallen and his boat was aground. Still infatuated, the rodents kept up their paddling until, one by one, they perished in the mud. The Pied Piper returned triumphant to the Town Hall to collect his £500.

However, no longer facing a desperate situation in their town, the burgesses now saw things in a different light. The need for economy was again paramount. Getting rid of the rats had proved a much easier task than imagined, they told the Piper, suggesting that £50 would be a more than ample reward. Incensed, the Piper demanded that the previously agreed sum be paid to him. When the Mayor refused, he left the Town Hall, swearing he would avenge this mean-spirited act. The Piper marched through the town as before, playing the same shrill tune on his pipe. Emerging from their homes, the people laughed, secure in the knowledge that all the rats were dead and none would be attracted by the music. But, while the Piper was ridiculed by the older folk, the children of the town ran after him, hopping and dancing to his irresistible music.

Down Silver Street he went, up Gold Street, then through an avenue of oaks outside the town. Soon, the shrill notes of his pipe died away in the distance. In Francheville the people awaited the return of their children. They waited in vain, for the Piper and the children were never seen again. Eventually, there came a time when the remaining inhabitants of Francheville had, inevitably, either died or become enfeebled with old age, while the children born since the Piper's visit were still infants. If legend is to believed, the French knew of this state of affairs when, in 1377, they launched a devastating attack on the Island's north-west coast. Francheville, its citizens unable to put up a fight, was burnt to the ground.

The usual way of rounding-off the Piper's tale is to point out that, from the ruins of Francheville, a 'new town' emerged – an irresistible origin for the present place-name. In fact, while it is true that the town was sacked by the French in 1377, and partially rebuilt some time afterwards, Newtown had been its name (alternative spellings included Newetone, le Neuton and le Nywetoune) for more than a century before the raid, alongside the original title of Francheville (a name which continued to be spasmodically used, in one spelling form or another, well into the sixteenth century). As for the Pied Piper, when Abraham Elder included the story in his *Tales and Legends of the Isle of Wight*, published in 1839, Browning had yet to popularise the Hamelin legend in his famous poem – although Elder did know of the Hamelin tale. Interestingly, the 'true' setting for the Browning poem has actually been identified by some writers as the Isle of Wight – but at New*port* rather than New*town*!

The most plausible origin for the original Piper tales is a connection with the Black Death, or some other dread disease spread by rats. It is a matter of record that the population of the Isle of Wight had been seriously reduced by the spread of plague in the fourteenth century. Francheville would not have escaped and, as a result, really would have been hard-pressed to defend itself against attack in 1377. The Piper may have sprung from the imagination – but the French really did call the tune at Francheville.

HEYNO'S SILVER BOW

Of the many raids launched against the Isle of Wight from the continent of Europe by an assortment of foes, it is the devastating French-led attack of 1377 which has most enriched the Island's treasure chest of country lore and traditions. Newtown's Pied Piper legend is but one of the numerous stories which have been told against the backdrop of the 1377 assault on the Island's north-west coast – and the subsequent siege and successful defence of the inland castle of Carisbrooke.

The Hundred Years' War with France was in mid-course, and the south of England still smarting from wounds inflicted by a wave of enemy attacks the previous month, when the Island was raided on 15 August. Having in quick succession laid waste to Yarmouth, nearby Francheville and finally Newport, a combined French and Spanish force then advanced on the defensive stronghold of Carisbrooke. They had landed in considerable numbers at Yarmouth and, although the Island had been on continuous invasion alert for some years, the raiders seem to have met little resistance, and suffered few casualties *en route* to the castle.

Their fortunes were to change dramatically at Carisbrooke. Easily and well defended, the castle proved impregnable, despite the enemy's repeated attempts to storm it. Indeed, if we accept the veracity of one of the most enduring stories from the period of the siege, the tables were savagely turned on the invaders when a party of them were ambushed in a narrow lane near the castle ramparts and mercilessly cut to pieces in an encounter which, according to some sources, Islanders were later to recall with glee as the Battle of the Noddies. The word 'noddy' may have been used on the Island as a term of abuse – meaning either an idiot or a dead body – and it is often suggested that Islanders reserved it particularly for the French. More likely is the optional explanation that it was used to denote places of noted slaughter. And, if the tradition of the ambush is based on fact, slaughter there most certainly was in that narrow lane north-east of the castle.

For centuries afterwards it was known as Deadman's Lane, until Admiral Nelson's own epic battle triumph of 1805 paved the way for its renaming in 1861 as Trafalgar Road. Or perhaps Deadman's Lane was so called because it was where the slaughtered enemy soldiers were buried – having actually been slain a few yards away in what became known as Noddies' Hill, later corrupted to Node Hill, until it, too, was renamed in 1861 (as Upper St. James' Street). Both theories have been put forward – and so has a third which locates slaughter and burial the other way round:

> The Frenchmen slain in Deadman's Lane:
> they lie on 'Noddies Hill,'
> Of Heyno's fame and raiders' shame
> there names bear witness still.

Whatever the truth, it is pleasing to record that, despite its official re-naming well over a century ago, the street name Node Hill continues in colloquial use to this day.

Carisbrooke Castle was commanded at the time of the siege by Sir Hugh Tyrell, then Captain of the Island, and he has justly gone down in history as the man who successfully led the resistance in what was only the second – and would turn out to be the last – taste of military action at the fortress. Yet, legend has greater respect for another's contribution to the defeat of the rampaging enemy at the door. The seventeenth century manuscripts of Sir John Oglander provide the essential facts:

> 'When ye Ffrench had taken ye Island and beseyghed Caresbroke Castle, one Petrus de Heynoe came to Sir Hugh Tyrell, then Captayne of the Island, and told him he would undertake with his sillver bowe to kill ye Commander of ye Ffrench, taking his time, for he had observed him how nyghtes and morninges he came neare ye Castle: which on leave he killed (him) owt of a loope-hole on ye west syde of ye Castle.'

Peter de Heyno, as he is more usually recalled (the Heyno referred to in the rhyme above), was lord of the manor of Stenbury, which lies between the villages of Wroxall and Whitwell in the south of the Island. At the time of the 1377 raid, he commanded one of the nine local militia, with responsibility for defending the Island's south-eastern coast from St. Catherine's to Culver Cliff – but it was at Carisbrooke that he carved his niche in history as arguably the Island's most charismatic hero. For that single lethal shot with the legendary silver bow deprived the invading force of their commander and seems to have left them utterly demoralised. They called off the siege, retreated to Yarmouth and left the shocked and devastated Isle of Wight to begin its long, painful recovery.

On Carisbrooke Castle's west side, the arrow slit from where Peter de Heyno is supposed to have taken aim with the silver bow is known to this day as 'Heynoe's Loope'.

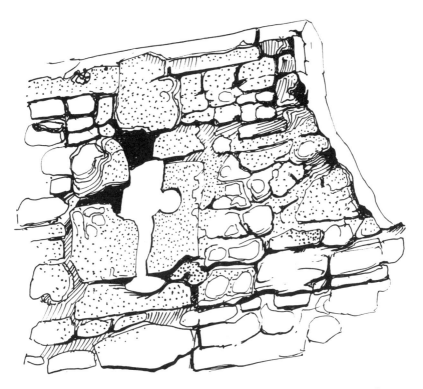

'Heynoe's Loope' at Carisbrooke Castle. It was from this slit, according to tradition, that Peter de Heyno(e) fired the decisive arrow which killed the French commander leading the siege against Carisbrooke Castle in 1377 and turned the tables on the invaders.

This is the Rime of the Silver Bow and the Lord of Stenbury.
Whose name and fame will live for aye in Island history.
Then health to the bow, and the archer bold and the bolt of the ashen tree,
The bolt that laid the Frenchman low and set our Island free.

So runs the opening to the song which records the heroic deed. Yet, in a final twist to the tale, setting the Island free was actually a costly affair. The invaders, we are told, were paid 1,000 marks to leave the Island – and not return. There again, other accounts suggest that the money transaction was the other way round, and that the French paid the Island ten times that amount to guarantee their safe passage!

A CURSE ON THE DUVER

The buttressed tower of the otherwise vanished Duver church clings determinedly to dry land by St. Helen's shore, stark remnant of a less than glorious chapter in the religious history of Wight. It is a curious location for a place of Christian worship, a reputedly haunted site with an abundance of legendary associations.

St. Helen's village owes its name to the dedication of the local priory to the Emperor Constantine's mother, St. Helen, in the closing years of the eleventh century. The area had been provided with its first place of worship – founded by Hiddila, chaplain to the missionary Bishop Wilfrid – nearly 400 years earlier. A wooden church, constructed near the sea on the sandy strip of land known today as The Duver (see the next chapter), it was eventually replaced in stone by the Cluniac monks at the priory. The new structure served both as a church for local worshippers and as a chapel for the monks themselves, who dedicated it to St. Helen.

Later alterations included the thirteenth century tower, much of which remains to this day, the mediaeval stonework of its landward face contrasting with the incongruity of white-painted Trinity House brickwork on the seaward side. The remainder of the church has long since been swept away by the sea. As early as the sixteenth century it was described by the diarist Sir John Oglander as being 'almost utterly decayed, so that one may look in at one end and out at the other, which causeth the whole realm to run in slander, for it joineth hard by the sea-side where all sorts of nations coming aland for water or vittals, seeing the shameful using of the same, think that all other churches within the realm be like used, and what they have said in their own country, God knoweth.'

The state of the church continued to cause alarm – national as well as local – as the years progressed, but little was done to halt its steady deterioration and gradual surrender to the sea. Its final collapse is attributed by local folklore to the great storm of 20 November 1703. It left intact little more than the tower which still stands on the very edge of the shore. This was subsequently bricked-up for use as a seamark, a function it continues to perform to this day, and a new parish church was built on an inland site in the eighteenth century.

However, thanks to the long-established use of St. Helen's as a safe

This delightful lithographed illustration of the old Duver Church at St. Helens was originally produced for Percy Stone's *Architectural Antiquities of the Isle of Wight* in 1891. Then, as now, only the tower remained of this cursed shore-side building.

anchorage for naval vessels, there was a further role for the fallen remains of the old Duver church. Sailors supposedly discovered that the stones of the wrecked building (possibly the churchyard tombstones as well) were ideal for scouring the decks of their ships; many were consequently plundered. Before long the task became known as 'holystoning' – an expression which persists to this day. This curiosity was recalled until recently by an explanatory sign on the church tower.

Another, much older, sign used to remind visitors that the small green immediately behind the tower was the site of the burial ground (a use it continued to perform for St. Helen's parish up until the eighteenth century). 'The sanctity of the churchyard should be respected,' read its message. However, it may be that a more powerful force commands respect here, for the misfortunes of the ill-starred Duver church have long been attributed to an evil curse.

From Hiddila's time, right up until the mid-eighteenth century, the church functioned without a parish priest. During this 500-year period it seems probable that the priory – in the shape of the Prior himself – filled the gap by taking on the priestly duties. Finally, in 1250, Philip de St. Helena (it was customary for priests to adopt the name of their place of domicile) was appointed to the job, probably remaining in post until the closing decade of the thirteenth century. It may be that a successor could not be found, for legend insists that it was in the early years of the fourteenth century that the monk Aymo, St. Helen's incumbent Prior at the time, was doubling as priest at the church.

Aymo, either through his actions or as a result of evil rumour, brought shame upon St. Helen's Church and Priory. It was said that he now worshipped not God, but the Devil, and that Satanic rites were performed on the altar of the church. A bestial coven of witches supposedly met there under his direction. Becoming increasingly deranged, Aymo defied excommunication by the religious authorities and continued to preach in the church, apparently unconcerned by the fact that he was splendidly alone in the place, the congregation having deserted it. These strange events seem to be the foundation for the curse which local people believed had settled on the church, and which proceeded to eat away at the very fabric of the building until it was all but washed into the sea.

The exception, of course, was the tower. In 1784 – the engraved date is still visible – workmen from Portsmouth arrived to strengthen its foundations and brick-up the seaward side. The final task, we are told, was the application of the white paint. As the foreman climbed a ladder either to start the job or to apply finishing touches to the paintwork – there is more than one version of this story – he was 'very much astonished,' in the words of Abraham Elder's version, to find 'a little old fashioned gentleman in tight leather shorts and black worsted stockings' asleep on top of the tower. The startled foreman summoned his colleagues.

Angered by the intrusion, the man cursed the work party, condemning them to suffer the same fate as an earlier party of masons who had laid the first stones of the tower – and had then disappeared on their return voyage to the mainland. Since he claimed to remember that incident, centuries before, the eighteenth century workmen regarded the old man's curse as a huge joke. He had mysteriously vanished from the tower-top by the time they packed up their tools and set sail for Portsmouth.

They were never seen again.

THE IDOL OF HOLY CROSS

Pretty she most certainly isn't. Neither is there anything remotely modest about her. Yet Binstead's oldest resident occupies an enduring place in the affections of her fellow villagers. In physical terms, her enduring occupancy is of a perch, in the form of a beast's head, above the keystone to the lower gate of Holy Cross churchyard. For want of a better name, generations have simply referred to her as 'the Idol'.

Calling this much-weathered ugly stone carving a 'her' may be regarded as something of an insult to womankind. Indeed, the Idol is usually referred to as an 'it'. However, noting a rather obvious feature of the feminine form when penning his classic history of the Island in the late-eighteenth century, Sir Richard Worsley had no hesitation in describing 'a woman figure'. Two centuries later, the writer Paul Hyland put it rather more graphically with his explicit pen-portrait of 'a grotesque, and bearded, *sheila-na-gig*, hands spreading her sex.' Hyland is not alone in suggesting that the Idol belongs to that distinctive class of enigmatic effigies (usually spelt *sheela-na-gig* by the Irish originators of the term), but there is much diversity of opinion about the precise origin and nature of the Binstead statue.

For a very long time, writers – and observers in general – have had just as much trouble in trying to work out the nature of the beast's head which serves as the Idol's perch.

The blocked Norman arch forming the gateway above which the Idol squats used to serve as the north entrance to the church's former nave centuries before Sir Thomas Hellyer's rebuilding of Holy Cross in the Early-English style in 1844. The arch was so positioned, though long since out of use, when Worsley put pen to paper in 1781, describing the Idol as 'sitting with feet on a kind of pedestal resembling a ram's head.' Charles Tomkins, writing in 1796, offered an alternative, detailing 'a rude figure sitting on a bracket which has the appearance of a horse's head.'

When Thomas Barber's *Picturesque Illustrations of the Isle of Wight*, published some 40 years later, had another stab at describing the 'rudely sculptured stone', by now moved to a new position above the door of the porch on the south side, the nature of the beast's head was changed yet again – and Barber also saw the Idol itself in a rather different light. It was, he wrote, 'plainly intended for a man, who appears seated with

The Idol of Holy Cross, much-weathered but surviving the centuries as
Binstead's most celebrated 'resident'.

his feet resting upon a dog's, or wolf's, head.' Writing in 1856, by which
time the Idol had assumed its present position on the churchyard
boundary, W. H. Davenport Adams offered his readers 'a roughly
shapen representation of the human demi-figure, supported on a ram's
head.' Today, the common consensus is that the Idol is indeed perched
on the head of a ram.

The bigger question – the origin of the Idol itself – continues to
puzzle. There is little doubt that the Norman arch is as old as any part
of the present church, and there is a school of thought which suggests
the odd little sculpture is a Norman ornamentation of the sort often

employed by the architects of the period for the keystones and friezes of their buildings. A tendency towards the grotesque was not uncommon. Outspokenly dismissive of any other possible explanation was Henry Penruddock (known to his eighteenth century readers as H.P.W.), who was certain the Idol was 'no more than a large, preposterous figure, fitting naked, which was, in the early and rude ages, considered as ornamental to some part of the building, and which absurd and barbarous taste actually continued in this country until the reign of Henry VII.'

However, most historians agree that, before the Normans built Holy Cross, there would have been a Saxon church on the site to serve the men who quarried the renowned Quarr-Binstead stone. So was the Idol a relic of that original structure? If that was the case, there is good reason to make the assumption that the old pagan beliefs were the dominating influence behind the carving – as its appearance firmly suggests.

Davenport Adams tells us that 'some have considered it the emblem of the great God Thor, the Jupiter of the Northern Religions ... or it may possibly have been intended as an emblem of Strength.' Other figures, similar in style and workmanship, were re-used in Hellyer's nineteenth century rebuilding: a dragon in the act of biting its waving tail, a symbol of Eternity; and symbolical illustrations of both Sin and – above the porch – the dove of the Sanctus Spiritus. But the more usual theory of pagan origin for Binstead's ancient Idol is that it represents a Mother Goddess, symbolising propagation or, perhaps, fertility.

Whatever the true meaning and origin of the sculpture – fitted with a protective triangular gable in the nineteenth century – it is now synonymous with Binstead and its church (which, in contrast to the Idol, is idyllically pretty). Down the ages, the local people have adopted an attitude of protective reverence towards their famous little sculpture. They protect her – and she protects them. Woe betide anyone who attempts to cause her harm – and woe betide the villagers if anyone succeeds.

In the eighteenth century, Albin's Isle of Wight history recounts, the church authorities decided to remove the Idol from sight. When they did so, there was an immediate outcry, and it was quickly restored. The exercise has never been repeated.

THE LEGEND OF
LUCY LIGHTFOOT

The legendary Lucy Lightfoot lived in both the fourteenth and nineteenth centuries, slipping through a time warp from the latter to the former during a great storm to be with the dashing Crusader whose striking effigy in Gatcombe Church she held in rapturous admiration. The tale is internationally-famous. The church guide book tells of the 'many visitors, some not anxious to disbelieve the story', who seek out the idyllically situated thirteenth century church of St. Olave in order to view the carved wooden effigy beneath an arch in the chancel. The same adjective is almost always used to describe the figure – 'enigmatic' – and not merely for the expressionless face. For the truth is that nobody really knows whom the effigy represents.

The legend ignores the puzzle. It confidently asserts that the life-sized figure, carved in solid oak, is that of Edward Estur, who left the Isle of Wight in 1364 to join the volunteers of Peter I, King of Cyprus, in his quest to shake the hold of the Mamelukes in the Holy Land. He was, the story recounts, a member of the Estur (originally Fitz Stur) family who acquired the manor of Gatcombe at the time of the Conquest. St. Olave's Church initially served as a chapel to the manor house.

In 1834, more than five centuries after Edward supposedly departed the isle on his gallant mission, the legend tells of a young woman from Bowcombe who took to worshipping at St. Olave's. 'She was a most attractive young person, vivacious and romantic in spirit, and a fearless horsewoman', wrote the Rev. James Evans, erstwhile Rector of Gatcombe, in a booklet first produced to aid church funds in the early 1960s. 'Her dark beauty and passionate nature captured the hearts of most of the young men in the district. Her talents were known far afield.' This was Lucy Lightfoot. 'Alas for her admirers,' added the Rector's tale, 'Lucy was quite indifferent to their advances. She had become infatuated, it seems, with the effigy of the manly and handsome Crusader. Often, she was seen to enter the church and stand in rapturous admiration, gazing at him with his shield and dagger.' In her thoughts and dreams, she would accompany him on his adventures.

The booklet provides us with a very clear picture of Lucy's background (she was a farmer's daughter who lived at Stoney Meadow

St. Olave's Church at Gatcombe, where the legendary Lucy Lightfoot slipped through a time warp to be with the man she loved.

Farm in the Bowcombe Valley) and of the extraordinary events of 13 June 1831, when she was seen to enter St. Olave's 'at about 10.30am after tethering her horse by the gate.' While she was in the church, a violent storm broke out, lasting about two hours, and accompanied by a total eclipse of the sun, beginning at 11 am and continuing for 40 minutes. Such a combination was unique on the Island. Considerable damage was caused. When it was over, and the Island struggled back to normality, the tale continues, 'farmer George Brewster from Chale' noticed a frightened and restive horse outside the gate to St. Olave's. Inside the church, however, there was no-one to be seen. Lucy Lightfoot had vanished – and she was never seen again.

However, according to Mr. Evans' extraordinarily detailed narrative, nineteenth century research later 'rediscovered' a young woman ('brave and beautiful') of the same name and from the same part of the Island, living some 500 years earlier as the lover and companion of Edward Estur at the time of his adventures in the Holy Land. To cut short a rather longer story, Edward's gallant military deeds in the cause of Christianity leave him deranged and with absolutely no memory of his relationship with Lucy. She subsequently marries a Corsican fisherman, lives to an advanced age and is 'mourned by her many children and grandchildren.'

James Evans ended his account of Lucy's fantastic legend by suggesting – in equally detailed terms, and with apparent scientific support – some form of time distortion as explanation for her mysterious disappearance and apparent 'reappearance' five centuries earlier alongside the man she had 'always longed to be with.'

For years, the story teased the imagination of all those who popped their coins into the box at St. Olave's and left this most peaceful of Island churches clutching a copy of 'the legend', but most of today's purchasers buy their copies in full knowledge of the truth of the matter – that there is none! The characters and events are mostly fictitious. The story is an ingenious fantasy. James Evans made it all up. Yet he made such a good job of it that it has acquired a certain dignity over the years and is now firmly established as folklore.

True mystery remains. The effigy is not a memorial to Edward Estur – there was no-one of that name – but it could have been carved in memory of a real member of the Estur family. It is apparently old enough. No written records survive to confirm this, and an optional explanation is that it actually represents Sir Ralph de Gorges, of Knighton, whose involvement with the Crusades of the thirteenth century, followed shortly by his death, is documented. The diligent research of historian Richard Frost suggests that it was taken to Gatcombe as extraordinary reparation for damage caused there in 1307 by a rampaging band of vandals led by the knight's grandson. The magnificently-carved effigy would certainly have been regarded as an object of value at the time, while Sir Ralph's membership of the mysterious Knights Templar may by then have become an embarrassment to his family.

There is further fascination at the feet of the cross-legged knight. Here lies a representation of small dog, which some have identified as the legendary Flacon-Caprice. If you call at St. Olave's on Midsummer Night you may see him in animated form as he dances in the moonlight and calls on the spirits to join him in merry churchyard revels. You may see him – but you won't catch a glimpse of Lucy Lightfoot.

THE PLAYGROUNDS
OF PUCK

If the little people thrive on the Isle of Wight there are two places where, surely, you will find them. It is irresistible to link both Puckpool Point, near Ryde, and Puckaster Cove, to the east of St. Catherine's Point, with the fairies. The very names suggest the playgrounds of mischievous sprites and it is, therefore, both surprising and disappointing that so few fairy tales associated with either place appear to have been written. It is, however, possible to find the odd example of writers yielding to the temptation and weaving intricate fairy stories around the Island haunts of Puck. How much tradition is associated with these tales is open to question.

Puckpool is a place-name which promises much yet delivers virtually nothing of legendary interest. The word has relatively recent origins and is probably a fanciful interpretation of Pouppoll, by which name this corner of north-east Wight was formerly called. Puckpool, however, had become well-established as the place-name by the time the point was transformed through the building of a 21-mortar battery between 1863 and 1865 as part of the nation's defences against feared attack by France. If Puckpool ever had been the 'resort of fairies' which some suggested, this development must have put paid to their revels for good. Yet, today, the battery-turned-park is again the haunt of the little people, a popular holiday playground with an assortment of attractions for children.

The small natural harbour of Puckaster Cove (where Charles II sought refuge from 'a great and dangerous storm' in 1675) has by far the greater claim to tradition. Options exist for the origin of the place-name – and options within options. According to some sources, it is a corruption of the name by which the Romans knew the place, and of the alternatives offered within this option, *Pudica Castra*, meaning an impregnable camp, seems to have as good a claim as any. It suggests former importance at Puckaster – though traditionally an importance established centuries before the Isle of Wight was taken for the Roman cause by Vespasian's 2nd Legion in 43 AD. The Romans may have given the area of the cove a name, but, if tradition is to believed, they inherited its key role in the lucrative tin trade which had been pursued by the ancient Britons as early as 300 BC.

[54]

Fishermen gaze out to sea in Thomas Barber's evocative early-nineteenth century engraving of Puckaster Cove. Tin may well have been the prominent trade here at one time – not to mention gold dust!

Cornish tin, we are told, was brought overland to Lepe, on the Hampshire shore, then transported across the Solent – possibly utilising a low tide causeway – to Gurnard, on the Isle of Wight's northern coast. From there, it was taken north-south across the Island to a tin mart at Niton and thence the short distance to Puckaster Cove, the – probably fortified – depot and embarkation point for the cross-Channel section of a trading route which would eventually cross France to reach the Mediterranean port of Marseilles, then return to the sea for the final leg to Rome itself. A fear of piracy on the wide stretch of open sea south of Cornwall is the reason usually suggested for the traders' adoption of the seemingly laborious route via the Isle of Wight rather than a more direct sea crossing to France.

To a large extent this is all conjecture and, indeed, it is dismissed as a 'preposterous' thesis by some sources. There is, however, physical evidence on the Island and elsewhere – the remains of trackways and archaeological finds in the relevant areas – to support the theory of the Isle of Wight tin trail. Which is rather more than can be said of Puckaster Cove's supposed involvement in another valuable commodity. Gold dust, to be precise. Writing in 1926, Ethel C. Hargrove told of the cove being 'particularly favoured by fairies, who used the seashore for their revels.' At midnight, 'Puck's little star' would shine brightly above the cove.

One day, two men were talking there. Said one to the other: 'You are going to build a house – choose the spot where the fairy rings are. Puck will not bewitch the children.' To which the other replied: 'I had better not interfere with the fairies.' Soon afterwards, following a wedding feast, the first man to have spoken had to return home by way of Puckaster Cove. He followed a light which, after taking him in the wrong direction, led him to a patch of smooth grass. Music was heard and, in the words of Ethel C. Hargrove, 'a multitude of the small people, with red and purple caps, asked him to join their dances.' He would not, and the fairies disappeared, returning with an acorn filled with brown powder. They chanted:

> Now, now
> I'll show you how
> We make the tall
> Grow small.
> Sit down
> Upon the ground.

Having done so, he followed the fairies' instructions to inhale the brown powder – and became smaller and smaller. Then the fairies danced round him in a ring until they were alarmed by 'a grey whiskered rat.' The diminished man hid from the creature, but the fairies summoned up the courage to chase it away. 'So,' the narrative continues, 'they all sat on puff-balls which burst and covered them with gold dust, with which Puck restored the man to his original stature.' The latter managed to take home some of the dust and no doubt told his neighbours all about his adventure. 'But the people who picked up the Puckaster puff-balls never found any more gold dust,' concludes this somewhat disjointed fairy tale.

What inspired Ethel Hargrove to this exercise in whimsical writing can only be guessed at. Did she base the tale on established folklore? Supporting references are, to say the least, hard to find, so maybe it simply sprung from an imagination fired by the evocative name of Puckaster Cove. Some 14 years after publication of the tale in *From England's Garden Island*, Helge Kokeritz produced his studiously definitive guide to Isle of Wight place-names. Puckaster, he surmised, may have been derived from a conjunction of the Old English 'puca' (goblin) and 'torr' (rock or hill). Fairy, sprite or goblin, Puck continues to draw logically illogical conclusions!

ST. CATHERINE'S
PEPPER POT

On the downs above St. Catherine's, the southern-most point in the Isle of Wight, the Pepper Pot stands alongside the Salt Cellar on a lofty table-top overlooking the English Channel. Both were conceived as lighthouses. Only the Pepper Pot (officially St. Catherine's Oratory), by far the older of the two, was completed. Reaching a height of a little over 35 feet, on land some 750 feet above sea level, this rocket-like buttressed tower is Britain's sole surviving medieval lighthouse, dating back to the early fourteenth century. This first light of St. Catherine's owes its origin to the legendary greed of one Walter de Godeton, a man who thought he had acquired a large stock of wine on the cheap . . . and ended up paying dearly for it.

The story – based on fact, but long enshrined in local folklore – opens on a wild winter's night in April 1313 when the storm-tossed merchant ship *Ste. Marie of Bayonne*, carrying a consignment of white wine from Tonnay, in Edward II's Duchy of Aquitaine, ran aground on the treacherous rocks of Atherfield Ledge, the northern extremity of Chale Bay. By good fortune, some, or possibly all, of the sailors escaped from the stricken vessel and came ashore on the Island. What happened next is, to an extent, a matter of legal record, but one complicated by conspiracy and false testament.

While the ship was wrecked, its eminently desirable cargo appears to have been entirely salvaged. Once the storm had subsided, the merchant, Remigius de Depe, and his crew returned to the wreck and retrieved all 174 casks of wine from its hold. Contemporary records initially suggest that prominent Islanders then seized the wine as 'wrecks of the sea' – as had long been the custom for lords of manors abutting the coast – while a dispute raged in the courts over the legal ownership of ship and cargo. Remigius de Depe, having claimed title to both, found himself temporarily imprisoned at Winchester, apparently the victim of a plot hatched in Newport by a group of men who claimed ownership for themselves!

While all this was taking place, the wine had been dispersed; inevitably, it went to the wealthier Islanders in the area. Walter de Godeton, who owned land in the manor of Chale (his name is recalled in present-day Gotten), snapped up no less than 53 casks – either by seizure or through purchase. How much time he was given to drink to his success at acquiring such a quantity of fine drink is not known, but it can't have been long before the white wine from Aquitaine had turned metaphorically sour in Walter's mouth. News of the trading in Chale Bay had reached a justices' inquiry and its conclusion was that the whole business was illegal.

Possibly because it was proving difficult to determine ownership, let alone complicity on the part of the merchants, the full force of the law was then brought to bear against those who had acquired the wine on the Island. They were successfully charged with illegally receiving the casks. Walter de Godeton, who had either bought or helped himself to easily the largest single haul, received the heaviest of the penalties. He was ordered to pay 227½ marks (the equivalent to several thousand pounds today) in the civil courts. This was either a fine or, as some sources suggest, remuneration for the wine's full value – a little under five marks a cask. The next bit of the story probably owes more to enduring local tradition than to hard facts. It insists that, if Walter de Godeton thought the financial penalty was an end to the matter, he was to be sadly disillusioned.

The ultimate owners of the wine eventually turned out to be the monastery of Livers, in Picardy, and sacrilege was now 'on the agenda'. Walter de Godeton found himself hauled before the ecclesiastical court in Rome, where he was severely admonished by the Pope, and ordered to atone for his sin by equipping the high downs above Chale with a lighthouse to warn mariners against disasters of a similar nature to that which had befallen the merchant ship from Aquitaine. Attached to the lighthouse, De Godeton was told, he should provide an oratory for a priest, who would both tend the light and say masses for the souls of those who perished in the sea below. According to Sir Richard Worsley's classic history of the Isle of Wight, by 1328 De Godeton had done as he was required.

There was possibly already a lighthouse on that lonely spot, for it has been recorded that a Walter de Langstrell occupied a hermitage there prior to 1312, and may well have used some form of primitive warning device to 'watch over' those in potential distress at sea. If so, it was rendered obsolete by Walter de Godeton's lighthouse and chapel, dedicated to St. Catherine, which for the next two centuries served its purpose well – or as well as the frequent mists on the downs allowed – and led to the re-naming of Chale Down itself, and the promontory below, after the saint.

However, Henry VIII's Reformation sequestered the meagre revenue

The distinctive 'Pepper Pot' on St. Catherine's Down, Britain's only surviving medieval lighthouse, is shown here as drawn in 1801, looking much as it does today. Chale's notorious 'Bay of Death' lies beneath it at the foot of the cliffs.

of the oratory some time after 1547. The solitary monk ceased his masses and left St. Catherine's and its light for the last time. His chapel was plundered for building stone (the only visible traces of it today are the marks of its pitched roof attachment to the east side of the surviving tower) and for nearly 300 years passing ships were left to the mercy of the treacherous rocks and shoals of what justifiably became known as the Bay of Death.

Finally, in 1785, an effort was made to rekindle the St. Catherine's light when Trinity House embarked on the building of a new lighthouse not far from De Godeton's octagonal tower. However, as the building work progressed, it became increasingly clear that the mists and fogs would render it virtually useless. The work was abandoned. The squat tower-base stands to this day, dubbed the Salt Cellar by local people, and very much the inferior lighthouse curiosity alongside De Godeton's Pepper Pot, which is rightly regarded as a national monument, in the care of the National Trust, and is a focal point for walkers on the downland trails.

Beneath them, at a much lower altitude immediately above St. Catherine's Point itself, the present-day successor to De Godeton's light maintains a constant watch over the mariners who sail past the Isle of Wight's Bay of Death.

THE LEGEND OF
KING'S QUAY

The Isle of Wight's strategic importance to the mother country, or, put another way, its obvious vulnerability to attack from Continental Europe, has for centuries been reflected by the number of visits made to its shores by kings and queens.

Occasionally, they also came for the peace and quiet of the place. That was probably the thinking behind King Æthelred's decision to spend the Christmas of 1013 on the Island, away from the trials and tribulations being heaped on his mainland domain by the rampaging Danish monarch, King Sweyn. Cnut, son of Sweyn, was on the Island in 1022 following his coronation as King of England, and Harold Godwin, last of the Anglo-Saxon kings, is said to have spent the entire summer of 1066 on Wight awaiting the expected invasion from Normandy – before he was forced to hurry north to counter first the invasion of Northumbria by his other rival to the English throne, Harold Hardrada of Norway.

That, in the sequence of notable royal visits, brings us to the early years of the thirteenth century, and King John's ill-fated expeditions to recapture lost possessions in France. We have reliable evidence that John arrived in Yarmouth at the end of May 1206 for a brief stay while in the process of assembling his fleet for La Rochelle. He was back in the town early in February 1214 *en route* for Poitou – and catastrophic defeat at the Battle of Bouvines. These are indisputable facts. King John's reputed return to the Isle of Wight in 1215, following his forced signing of Magna Carta at Runnymede, is more the stuff of legend.

John regarded the Runnymede agreement as no more than a means of buying time in his struggle to defeat rebellion in England. He is said to have withdrawn rapidly from Kent to Southampton, from where he sent letters to trusted followers, imploring them to fortify their castles in his cause, and endeavoured to rally the military support of mercenary forces in Germany, France and Flanders. Then, we are told, he secretly crossed to the Isle of Wight, remaining for three months in something of a sulk while he continued to plot against the rebel barons. His disembarkation point on the north coast of the Island is said to have been the inlet, not far from present-day Wootton, which for centuries

The landing place at King's Quay. Whether King John landed here in 1215, as legend dictates, is probably a matter for whimsical conjecture – yet no other explanation for the name of the quay has ever been offered.

has been known as King's Quay. While on the Island, according to the writings of Roger de Wendover, John led 'a solitarie lyfe among reivers (pirates) and fishermen.'

If John did flee to the Island, the move was not without risk. Wight at that time was governed by William de Vernon, who had been a close ally of the late Richard I, John's brother and his predecessor on the English throne. Nothing could have guaranteed more animosity for de Vernon at the hands of the tyrannical John – and so it proved. William de Vernon paid dearly for his loyalty to the Lionheart; he was forced by King John to forfeit 500 marks and surrender his grandson, as a hostage, to the monarch's keeping. Odd, then, that the King should apparently later regard De Vernon's domain as a safe retreat in the aftermath of Magna Carta. If the visit did take place, John may have relied on the chivalrous nature of De Vernon for his safety. More likely, perhaps, he feared so greatly for his safety that he stayed well out of De Vernon's way. For the story goes that the King, in constant disguise, never strayed far from the coast and a quick means of escape.

Lurking, we are told, in the woods sloping to the shore on the Island's north-east coast, his true identity kept secret from the local people, John pondered on revenge. However, according to a particularly colourful version of the King's Quay legend, he did, albeit fleetingly, have something else on his mind. The story goes that he fell in love with a noble lady he chanced to meet one day as, sitting on the trunk of a tree, she caressed a greyhound. The lady shrank from John's initial advances, so he felt compelled to tell her that he was King of England. Her response was not the one for which he had hoped. 'Avaunt, villain,' she cried, 'Isobel de Rosco fears you not. Let me pass on my way.'

When King John persisted in his attempts to detain her, Isobel clapped her hands to summon her retainers, who quickly drew near. This formidable lady then threatened to hang the King from a tree, but eventually told him to go on his way and, in future, mind his manners! John did as he was told – but he was not the sort of man to let it lie there. Perhaps employing the talents of piratical Island friends in support, he proceeded to raid Isobel's home and take her prisoner. As might be expected, she managed to escape, and this extraordinary legend fizzles out the next morning with King John's return to the mainland for the last year of a less than glorious life, which ended in October 1216.

While it is not inconceivable that King John really did cross to the Island at this low point in his fortunes (though the stories of him temporarily turning merchant, fisherman or pirate were surely the inventions of his enemies), present-day thinking tends towards an apocryphal origin. This was not the case early in the ninteenth century. *Barber's Picturesque Illustrations of the Isle of Wight*, for example, recorded John's visit as – so far as the Island was concerned – perhaps 'the most remarkable historical fact connected with the Norman period.' It is also worth noting that no other explanation for the origin of the name King's Quay seems ever to have been put forward.

THE KING OF THE WIGHT

Those who take refreshment at The Bugle in either Brading or Yarmouth may wonder why these inns – and those of the same name which formerly existed in Carisbrooke, Newport (a recent loss) and Ryde – were so called. They may, logically, guess at some connection with the musical instrument; the inn sign at Yarmouth suggests precisely that. But such a guess, according to tradition, would be hitting the wrong note altogether. Bugle (from the Latin, *buculus*) is an alternative term for a young bull – the creature which proudly adorns the inn sign at the Brading hostelry. The word was commonly used on the Isle of Wight, and this, according to that expert on local dialect, W. H. Long, was the reason there were so many inns of the name on the Island – yet comparatively few elsewhere.

Well, part of the reason, perhaps. Long – and others – also suggest that it could be a legacy of the bizarre fifteenth century reign of King Henry I. That's not Henry I of England, incidentally. The fifteenth century Henry I enjoyed a short-lived reign in the 1440's. His domain? The Isle of Wight.

This was Henry Beauchamp, Duke of Warwick, the only crowned monarch the Isle of Wight has ever been able to claim all to itself. It is, unlikely, however, that anyone on the Island actually bothered to claim young Beauchamp as their own. He was foisted upon them for no other reason than his favoured status at the court of the King of England, Henry VI, who crowned Beauchamp King of the Wight with his own hands. Apart from demonstrating the English monarch's affection for Beauchamp, the latter's accession to the throne of Wight was a meaningless act. The Island's Lordship and government was in the capable hands of Humphrey, Duke of Gloucester – Henry VI's uncle – at the time and there was simply no role for Beauchamp in his offshore kingdom. Neither was there anything in the English constitution which allowed for a King of the Wight.

Beauchamp was the son of Richard, 5th Earl of Warwick and former Regent of France. Fourteen at the time of his father's death at Rouen in 1439, he was probably 18 (though some sources suggest he may have been two or three years older than that) when the gift of the Island's kingship was bestowed upon him. It was followed quickly by his elevation to the status of Premier Earl of England. Beauchamp's feeble constitution – he was said to be lacking, both in mind and body –

ensured that he would not be around very long to enjoy the fruits – whatever they were – of his titles and standing. He died in 1446 at his castle in Worcestershire when he was just 22 years old and was buried at the monastery of Tewkesbury, his unique reign as King of the Wight having lasted four years at the most.

During that period, Henry Beauchamp almost certainly never set foot on the Isle of Wight. It was probably a prudent decision. By all accounts, his coronation had not gone down well among the Island's leading inhabitants, no doubt confused and angered by the blatantly illegal act. History does not record what the Duke of Gloucester thought of the situation; we can safely assume he was not impressed.

It has been suggested that Henry VI's decision to bestow the Kingship of Wight upon Beauchamp was the action of a man whose own mental state was some way short of stable. However, there is general agreement that King Henry's well-documented slide into mental and physical collapse (from which he may never have recovered) immediately followed, and may well have been a direct consequence of, the disastrous defeat at Castillon in July 1453, which led to the loss of all remaining English-held territories in France with the solitary exception of Calais. This, of course, was some years after Beauchamp's death. So we can assume that Henry VI was perfectly sane and – as usual – well intentioned when he crowned his favourite as King of Wight. He was simply lacking in good judgment.

But how does the story of Henry Beauchamp relate to the naming of so many Isle of Wight inns after the bugle?

Beauchamp's coat of arms included a 'supporter' in the shape of a young bull and the suggestion is that his association with Wight led to the proliferation of Bugle inns on the Island. Just why the people of the Isle of Wight should choose to remember with such apparent affection the 'king' they never saw – and who could never have been more than an annoying irrelevance – is a mite puzzling.

In fact, it was another Beauchamp – Henry's grandfather, Thomas – who possibly made more of a mark on the Island. Thomas, Earl of Warwick, was apprehended in 1397 for his part in the Fitzalan Conspiracy, which aimed to imprison King Richard II and his friends. As punishments go, Warwick's was not bad at all. It certainly compared favourably with the fate of fellow conspirators the Earl of Arundel, executed on the King's orders, and the Duke of Gloucester, who was famously murdered by Richard. For Warwick, and later the Earls of Derby and Nottingham, the sentence was more lenient – exile in all three cases. Warwick's past services to the Crown, together with his advanced age (58), were mitigating factors.

BUGLE HOTEL

Yarmouth's Bugle Hotel features both the musical instrument of that name and a young bull on its distinctive inn sign. The Bugle at Brading, which also features a bull on its sign, is the only other surviving hostelry of that name on the Island. Others formerly existed in Newport, Carisbrooke and Ryde.

And to where was he exiled? According to some sources, Warwick was told: 'It is ordered that you banish yourself to the Isle of Wight, taking with you a sufficiency of wealth to support your state as long as you shall live, and that you never quit the Island.' Not at all displeased, we are told that Warwick thanked the King and Council for their leniency and promptly made the necessary arrangements to cross the Solent with part of his household, presumably surrendering (as a very privileged prisoner) to the castle of Carisbrooke. Richard's dethronement in 1399 probably brought the banishment – whether it really was served out on the Isle of Wight or elsewhere – to an early conclusion. Two years later Warwick was dead.

TRAGEDY IN THE TOWN

A tablet above the entrance to Newport's most distinctive restaurant bears the date 1701. Yet it is for the events of May 1584 that this fascinating town centre building is locally famous. The tablet also carries the inscription: 'God's Providence is my Inheritance'. From this, God's Providence House takes its name – and a distinction shared with similarly-inscribed houses in other parts of England. According to tradition, God's Providence is where the plague finally called a halt in Newport after eighteen unremitting months of human suffering and loss.

For this to be true, of course, the house in St. Thomas' Square would either have to be much older than the tablet suggests or a replacement for an earlier building. Probably, the truth lies in between. The present appearance of the house may date from 1701, but there is documented evidence to suggest only a partial rebuild in that year. Whatever the precise details of construction and reconstruction, there was certainly a house on the site in the sixteenth century – standing at what was then the junction between Pyle Street and the top (south) end of Holyrood Street.

It would have been standing when the Island's capital, periodically revisited by bubonic plague since the days of the Black Death two centuries earlier, recorded the much-feared return of the pestilence towards the end of 1582. This virulent outbreak raged throughout 1583 and well into the following year. It claimed the lives of more than 200 people and made development of the town's first burial ground at Church Litten – the distinctive stone archway remains to this day – an absolute necessity. Finally, during the second week of May 1584, the last of the deaths attributed to the loathsome epidemic was reported to the town authorities. The records they kept reveal that 'at Mr. Tuttiot's house ceased the plage, and God, of his mercy, toke ye plage from the Towne to our great comfortt, praysed be to his holy name, therefore, Amen.' The location of Mr. Tuttiot's home is not given, but tradition assumes that it was the house in Pyle Street, named God's Providence when later rebuilt in recognition of its role in the plague's demise.

It does not seem too fanciful a suggestion. Newport historian R.J. Eldridge has pointed out that, many years after the 1583-84 plague, a Dr. Tuttiet lived in Pyle Street. Notwithstanding the slight variation in spelling, was the Mr. Tuttiot whose house was immortalised in the 1584 Newport records an ancestor of the doctor's? If so, it would be reasonable to assume that he, too, had lived in Pyle Street.

Yet, this explanation for the naming of God's Providence House is just one option. Another insists that, rather than being the last home to record a plague death in 1584, the house was one of the very few in the town – possibly the only one – in which *nobody* died from the plague. If this is right, then the theory about Mr. Tuttiott's home being on the site of God's Providence House seems to fall flat. Whatever the precise facts, the architectural gem that is God's Providence House remains a prominent reminder of an awful chapter in the history of Newport.

Holyrood Street was first known as 'The Street that leads to St. Cross'. The building that stands at the opposite (northern) end to God's Providence House serves as a reminder of an even older – but equally tragic – chapter in the chronicles of the capital. St. Cross Court, an attractive modern block of sheltered housing for the elderly, is not historically interesting in itself, but its well-chosen, imaginative name recalls highly respectable antiquity, drama – and curious tradition.

This site, beside the River Medina's Lukely Brook tributary, was originally occupied by the twelfth century Priory of St. Cross, which seems to have been a possession of the French Abbey of Tirone. Older even than Newport itself – it was built before 1120 – the Priory spawned a mill and prospered with the developing town before Frenchmen of a different ilk to those who had founded the place arrived there in 1377. In laying waste to the town – which was totally uninhabitable for years – the French raiders also burnt down St. Cross Priory and its mill. Both were later rebuilt, but the Priory never fully recovered its prosperity.

Recovery, according to legend, was beyond one unfortunate monk of St. Cross, whose throat was fatally slit by a fellow brother after a fierce quarrel. The weapon, so the story goes, was a pair of scissors, which the murderer dropped onto a flagstone after committing the crime. As a penance, he was given the task of obliterating the bloodstains which stubbornly adhered to the stone. Scrub as he might, he could never remove them. In time, on the dissolution of the religious houses, the Priory passed to the ownership of Winchester College and the site was later redeveloped as a private dwelling – St. Cross House. Here, the legend picks up again.

It is said that the flagstone – still carrying the bloodstains from the medieval murder – formed part of the floor of a passage at St. Cross House. When the building was demolished in the 1880s to make way for the construction of the Freshwater, Yarmouth and Newport Railway, the celebrated flagstone was rescued and preserved. For years, we are

God's Providence House, one of the most historically fascinating buildings in Newport. This postcard from the 1950s was illustrated by the well-known Island artist and caricaturist Tom Smitch. The restaurant has changed little in the intervening years.

told, it was exhibited at Mr. Ledicott's antique shop at the corner of Crocker Street. The infamous stains could still plainly be seen.

This tradition is one of many associated with St. Cross. During the eighteenth century, General Wolfe is said to have slept at the house before his tragically heroic assault on Quebec during the Seven Years War with France. In the same century, during a ball at St. Cross, part of the floor gave way and some of the guests fell into a cellar which nobody knew was there. In it were found the massive oak doors of the former monastery – later turned into tables – although the discovery in a chimney of the old monastery bell was not made until the house's demolition.

A STREAM OF TRADITION

Why Ryde? It is something of a sad irony that the geographical feature which almost certainly provided the origin for this intriguing place-name has been largely consigned to subterranean insignificance by the development of the very town it helped to create. Monktonmead Brook is the stream after which, it is usually suggested, the original fishing hamlet in the vicinity of its exit point to the Solent was named. In Old English, a small stream was known as a 'rith' (pronounced rithe).

Interestingly, although several variations of the name have been in use both before and since – la Riche, la Rye and la Ride are three examples – there are documented references to la Ryde as early as the thirteenth century, when it was part of the old manor of Ashey. By the fifteenth century, the French article 'la' had been largely dropped from the title. So Ryde was known as such centuries before Victorian development transformed the place – and buried the brook.

But only in the town itself. This northern reach of Smallbrook's rural stream, known as Monken Mede brook when it formed Ashey's eastern manorial boundary, can still be traced as it accompanies the railway line from Brading – first on its western side, then, after St. John's Road station, on the eastern – into Ryde. It then disappears from view to run ingloriously beneath the town and its Esplanade before reaching the sea just west of the swimming pool and boating lake. Prior to the extensive Victorian development, the brook had no need to burrow underground as it meandered towards journey's end at the duver (the local name for a sandy strip of coastal land – still recalled in the present-day name of Dover Street).

Monken Mede itself was composed of just under six acres of meadow beside the brook, belonging to the Cistercian monks at Quarr Abbey, two miles to the east, who acquired the land in the twelfth century. That explains the name – but there is a greater fascination connected with the brook-side meadows. Tradition asserts that an Abbot of Quarr used regularly to visit a family who tenanted the abbey's Ninham (Newnham) grange. Grateful for the cordial hospitality always extended to him – and to his horse – by the tenant's family, he bequeathed to successive Ninham tenants the first crop of hay which Monken Mede produced in alternate years. In return, the tenants were required to preserve a stone image at the grange.

East Ashey Manor House. The manor once included the whole of present-day Ryde and dispensed justice through its own manorial courts system – the Court Leet, Court Baron and View of Frank Pledge.

The custom seems to have been observed for several centuries. Remarkably, there are references to it as late as 1826 – even though Quarr's ownership of the meadows had ceased (along with the original abbey itself) hundreds of years before. The first crop of hay produced on the meadows was reaped not by the landowner, nor by anyone renting the land from him, but by the occupants of Newnham Farm, some two miles away and with no formal connection whatsoever with the land!

A modern-day reminder of the monk's former ownership of the meadowland is provided not only by the partially-buried brook, but also by Monkton Street, which parallels Monktonmead Brook – on the other side of the railway line – as the stream runs northwards from St. John's Road station and disappears beneath ground.

Long before the development of Ryde, Monktonmead Brook served as the eastern boundary for the manor of Ashey, the history of which is also linked to a religious community – but nuns rather than monks in this case. Ashey was given to the Abbey of Wherwell, near Andover, Hants, in the thirteenth century. The nuns established a cell at what is now East Ashey Manor Farm and the manor remained in their ownership until dissolution in the reign of Henry VIII, when it was acquired by Giles Worsley, who had been leasing it from the Abbess.

And that brings us to the second of the Monktonmead traditions. According to an enduring account, it was the nuns of Ashey who were responsible for the naming of the neighbouring Domesday manor of Nonoelle (present-day Nunwell). They were said to regularly resort to the latter's clear spring waters (the waters of Monktonmead) to replenish the supply at the nunnery. Irresistibly tempting though it may be to link the nuns to the stream which rises near Nunwell Farm and, thereby, to the origin of Nunwell's name, this may just be a little too good to be true. What is undisputed is that, prior to 1522, the manor house at Nunwell – which had been attacked and burnt by the French in a fourteenth century raid – was further west than the present building, confusingly close to East Ashey Manor, beside the stream. The old earthworks can still be seen.

Another historical fact – confirmed by manorial records – which touches on custom and tradition is an incident which somewhat detracts from East Ashey's religious associations. During the reign of Elizabeth I an unfortunate widow by the name of Agnes Porter, living within the jurisdiction of the Lord of the Manor, was accused of practising witchcraft and found guilty. Forfeit of all her goods and chattels to the Lord of Manor was one part of the punishment meted out. The other underlined the superstition-fuelled cruelty of the age. She was burnt at the stake.

THE STIRRING TALE OF
HOBBY HOBSON

In the short reign of Queen Anne at the beginning of the eighteenth century 'Hobby' Hobson carved for himself a permanent niche in the folklore of the Isle of Wight. His oft-recounted story is a classic tale of the local lad made good ... the 'prentice-boy from Niton who ran away to sea and eventually became one of the most celebrated sea-dogs of his time, ending his career as both an admiral and a knight.

Hobson, so the story goes, was a young orphan when he was apprenticed by the parish of Bonchurch to a tailor at Niton, some five miles away. This was a stroke of good fortune for young Hobby (or Jack, as some accounts have it) for he was accepted by the tailor's family as one of their own. One day, he was seated on his master's shop-board when a squadron of English men o' war was spotted passing the Island's south-western coast. In common with virtually everyone else in the village, Hobby ran down to the beach to view the spectacle. He was singularly impressed.

In a moment of youthful enthusiasm, the tailor's apprentice took a small boat that had been beached on the shore and rowed towards the squadron. It must have been a struggle, but he managed to safely reach the flagship, commanded by an admiral, and was accepted on board as a volunteer. Hobby had cast his rowing boat adrift; in his excitement he had also left his hat on the shore. When both were eventually retrieved, the Niton villagers understandably concluded that poor Hobby had met with a watery grave. Nothing could have been further from the truth.

The day after Hobby joined the squadron, it was involved in fierce action with a French fleet. We are told that the ships of the two opposing admirals were locked yard-arm to yard-arm, and both were obscured in smoke. Victory for either side was doubtful at this stage. Hobby had cheerfully played his part in two hours of fighting when, growing a little impatient, he enquired of an experienced sailor how much longer the action was likely to last, and how it would be concluded. On being told that the engagement would be won when the white 'rag' was struck (removed) from the enemy flagship's masthead, Hobby exclaimed: 'Oh! If that's all, I'll see what I can do.' Using the cover provided by the dense smoke, he set about the capture of the enemy flag ... with his own hands!

Hobby used the rigging of his ship to reach that of the French ship via the main-yard. Then, unseen, he proceeded to climb to the main-top-gallant masthead, remove the flag and return by the same route to the comparative safety of the English flagship. The disappearance of the 'rag' was soon noticed. 'Victory!' shouted the English tars. On the French ship, confusion reigned. Before her officers could restore order, the English sailors swarmed aboard to put the contest beyond all doubt. At this point, to the astonishment of his colleagues, Hobson clambered down from the rigging to the main-deck with the French flag wound around his arm. He was quickly summoned to the quarter-deck.

It was, to say the least, an unusual way of 'striking the flag' and winning a battle. Several of the ship's officers made clear their disapproval, but, fortunately for Hobby, the admiral saw things differently. Yesterday's tailor's apprentice was immediately promoted to midshipman, and an illustrious career at sea was under way. Hobson, the story continues, rose rapidly in his new profession until he was eventually made an admiral, and was then knighted by Queen Anne for the celebrated and oft-recounted feat of breaking through the Vigo Bay boom in 1702.

At some stage, the story switches back to the Isle of Wight. We are told how a party of naval officers arrived in Niton village and stopped at the 'humble door' of the house in which the tailor and his wife still lived. To the couple's astonishment, and probable dismay, they asked to be accommodated with such plain fare as could be prepared for them. The bacon and eggs they provided were liberally washed down with the fine wine the officers had brought with them. As the wine flowed, the conversation became the more animated.

This was particularly true of the leader of the officers' party. Addressing himself principally to the tailor's wife, he began dropping all manner of indirect hints as to his identity and youth. Having failed totally in this endeavour, he then started to sing her a verse from a ballad which had often been sung in her presence by the tailor's former 'prentice-boy. 'For all the world like our poor Hobby!' she exclaimed, tears streaming from her eyes. Admiral Hobson then put the couple out of their misery by revealing his true identity, and it is supposed the tailor and his wife were left that day significantly better off – in every sense – than they had been prior to the return of 'poor Hobby'.

The story has no doubt become the better for its repeated telling down the years. In all probability, Hobson's nickname (and the optional 'Admiral Snip', which recalled his supposedly humble origins) was actually added, to aid the narrative flow, long after the events described.

Sir Thomas Hopsonn (1642-1717), assumed to be 'Hobby' Hobson,
the 'prentice boy from Niton.

The fact is that there is no Admiral Sir Jack (or anything else) Hobson in the relevant naval lists. There is, however, a Vice-Admiral Sir Thomas Hopson (or Hopsonn), who lived from 1642 to 1717. It is he who is credited with leading the successful assault in October 1702 on the boom laid across the entrance to Redondela Harbour, on the west coast of Galicia, during a combined Anglo-Dutch raid on the Spanish treasure ships sheltering in Vigo Bay at the beginning of the War of Spanish Succession. His subsequent knighthood certainly seems to have been directly linked to the achievement.

So was Sir Thomas the former 'prentice-boy from Niton? Not according to the parish records at Shalfleet, some miles to the north-west, which register the birth there of Thomas Hopsonne, son of Captain Antony Hopsonne, on 6th April 1643. History formally accepts this as the true origin of the Vice-Admiral. The story of 'Hobby' Hobson seems a classic case of never letting the facts stand in the way of a good yarn!

GEORGE'S BRUSH WITH THE LAW

The story of the artist George Morland's arrest at Yarmouth, Isle of Wight, in 1799 as a suspected spy for Napoleon Bonaparte's France was extraordinary enough when presented in its factual form. As with all good tales, it tended to get better in the telling until fact and probable myth combined to endow it with legendary qualities.

Morland's skill with the paintbrush was not matched by his handling of financial matters. In 1799, heavily in debt, he seized the chance to escape the clutches of his many creditors in London by accepting the invitation of a friend, a Westminster surgeon named Lynn, to stay at the latter's Isle of Wight cottage in Cowes. Morland's ailing wife travelled ahead to Lynn's cottage in the April 'for the more speedy recovery of her health,' according to one of Morland's several biographers. The artist soon followed, accompanied by his servant, Sympson (or Klob, as some accounts have it). It was not the only visit made by George Morland to the Island, but it was destined to be the most memorable . . . and anything but a peaceful sojourn.

Not known for keeping the best of company, Morland attracted a motley collection of sailors, fishermen and smugglers to the rooms in which he painted at Cowes. It was not the ideal way of keeping a low profile, and news of his whereabouts soon reached London. By chance, the artist's brother, Henry, happened to be sitting in the White Horse pub in Fetters Lane when he overhead a group of Morland's creditors anticipating the flushing-out of George from his Island hideaway. Henry rode at speed to Southampton and crossed the Solent in time to warn his brother that the bailiffs were on his trail. So George Morland fled to Yarmouth, in the west of the Island. This was not one of his better decisions.

It seems he stayed with Henry and Sympson in the house of George Cole, a wealthy local smuggler. If a popular version of the story is to be believed, Morland then moved to the George Inn, where he struck up a friendship with the landlord, a Mr. Plumbly. While there, the artist's quiet sketching in the Square aroused suspicion – possibly because of his proximity to the then-fortified Yarmouth Castle – and one morning at breakfast he found himself arrested, along with Henry and Sympson, as a suspected enemy spy, on the orders of the local military commander.

The arrest was undertaken by a Lieutenant Don and eight soldiers of the Dorset Militia, who proceeded to march the perplexed trio the twelve miles to Newport on an uncomfortably hot day, to the accompaniment of jeers, cries of 'traitors!' and general abuse from the local people. Exhausted and agitated, they arrived in the Island's capital for an appearance before the Bench of Justices. The prosecution, if we are to believe the popular version of the tale, built its case around a drawing found on Morland when he was arrested. Since he was something of a specialist at painting animals, it should have come as no surprise that it was an unfinished sketch of a spaniel. The prosecution saw it differently, suggesting that it was a cunningly disguised map of the Isle of Wight! Morland was also accused of making a plan of Yarmouth Castle for the benefit of the enemy.

Things looked bleak, but help was on its way. Legend has it that Plumbly, Morland's landlord at the George, had been alerted to the artist's plight. In all haste, he rode from Yarmouth to Newport – jumping all 52 gates *en route* without stopping once – and arrived at the courtroom just in time to intercede on Morland's behalf. Plumbly's testimony carried some weight as, apart from his innkeeper's role, he was also Captain of the Isle of Wight Volunteers. As a result of this intervention, Morland and his companions were released, but the artist was warned against any further sketching while on the Island.

Rather less colourful are the accounts given by some Morland biographers which tell of Lynn arranging for George, on his arrival in the Island, to hand an introductory letter to a friend of the surgeon's who lived in Newport. This man was persuaded to purchase drawings from Morland on a regular basis. The arrangement was clearly against his better judgment, for he was soon complaining that the pictures he was expected to purchase were 'mere scratches with a pencil upon scraps of paper,' and he could 'buy better for 3d each at any of the shops in Newport!' He was probably glad to see the back of Morland when the artist fled to Yarmouth – but he was soon to prove a friend indeed.

According to these accounts of Morland's extraordinary Isle of Wight adventure, it was this same Newport benefactor who came to the aid of the artist and his companions at the court hearing, and secured their release. If this was the case, then Plumbly's legendary dash from Yarmouth must be regarded as just that – a legend – and neither it seems should we place too much faith in the story of the spaniel sketch. Herbert Baily's biographical essay, for example, refers only to suspicions being aroused by Morland's sketches of Yarmouth Harbour 'and other works . . . at a time when French invasion was dreaded.'

A delightful study of the profligate yet hugely talented George Morland,
as seen by Rowlandson.

George Morland could be justly accused of many things – his debts were largely the result of a dissolute lifestyle – but the charge that he was spying for the French was almost certainly without foundation. Baily adds that the whole episode later gave the artist 'the opportunity of hearty laughter, but at the time frightened him seriously.' It appears, however, that he did not take too seriously the Newport magistrates' warning against further sketching. He remained on the Island for some time after the 'spying' episode and painted two fine pictures – of the Needles and Freshwater Gate – before returning to the mainland in November.

THE KNIGHTEN COURT

Almost certainly unique to the Isle of Wight was the judicial tribunal which tradition asserts was set up by the Island's first Norman ruler, William FitzOsbern, as a means of keeping the vanquished Islanders in check and preventing rebellion. It was originally titled the *Curia Militem*, or Knights' Court, but has been mainly recorded as the Knighten Court. As such, albeit in considerably watered-down form, it dispensed justice for a remarkable eight centuries. As an established Isle of Wight custom, the Knighten Court had few, if any, equals.

The legal right and ability to summon such a tribunal was a significant privilege which underlines the considerable extent of self-government allowed by William the Conqueror to FitzOsbern, his brother-in-arms and most trusted military advisor, in the post-Conquest period. A tool of the feudal system under which the Island found itself governed by the Normans, the Knighten Court sat without a jury. Its judges were chosen originally from those holding a knight's fee in full or part (in effect, those who held land) from FitzOsbern and his successors as Lord of the Island.

Attendance at courts of justice was a common requirement for landholders throughout Norman England – part and parcel of the vow of allegiance and service sworn to the King in exchange for their land. On the Isle of Wight, however, allegiance was owed to the all-powerful Lord of the Island, rather than to the King of England. The Norman Lords received 15½ knight's fees – equal to 4,650 acres – from the Island's landholders, and it was at the court set up by FitzOsbern that the men who paid it were required to dispense justice.

Apart from swearing in the High Constables of the West and East Medyne, the two 'hundreds' into which the Island was divided for administrative purposes, plus the Tythingmen to preside over village communities – groupings of ten families made up a tythe; ten tythes equalled a hundred – history is obscure as to the extent of the Knighten Court's original powers under the harsh Norman system of justice. It is probably safe to assume that it was considerable and allowed the handing-down of the most severe penalties on a wide range of offences.

This had certainly been tempered by the early seventeenth century, from which period a very precise description of the Court and its activities has survived. Study of this fascinating document reveals that the practices of the Court at that time were probably those that had been in force for a very long period – though by now its pleadings and proceedings were subject to English law.

In their report of August 1626 to the then Governor of the Isle of Wight, Lord Conway, the gentlemen of the Island provided not only a comprehensive summary of the Court's powers, but suggested modifications aimed at increasing its effectiveness. By then, the report makes clear, the Knighten Court was summoned by the Steward to the Captain of the Island (successor to the Norman Lords) and held at the Town Hall in Newport on every third Monday – unless that happened to clash with a feast day, in which case the Court was adjourned for six weeks. The Court held jurisdiction throughout the Island, with the exception of the corporation of Newport itself. It dealt with cases of replevin (a writ to recover goods) and in actions of debt and trespass under the value of 40 shillings (£2).

The signatories to the 1626 report were unimpressed with the calibre of the Island freeholders who by then were dispensing the Court's justice. '. . . which freeholders,' they wrote, 'have been appointed by the captain of the isle to sit by four or five at a court by turns; but some being aged and impotent, one under age, some live out of the isle, and some of the rest being negligent of that service, there hath been much defected in their attendance; which is to the great prejudice of the court, and hindrance of the people, by the delay of trials.' The report's authors suggested electing additional judges from 'other sufficient men of the country' and imposing strict rules of attendance. They also sought powers for the court to deal with larger sums and, bearing this in mind, urged that a jury should be appointed.

Conway recognised the report's undoubted merit but, unlike William FitzOsbern almost 600 years earlier, he was powerless to implement the reforms called for. The document was forwarded to London, where it found favour at the highest level. However, although the Attorney General was directed to take the steps necessary to enlarge the jurisdiction of the Knighten Court, 'to all cases whichsoever, civil or criminal, under the value of £20, provided that the same extend not to the life, member or freehold of any of the inhabitants,' the reforms were never put in place. Amazingly, this unique Isle of Wight institution (which boasted a triple-towered castle as its distinctive common seal) was instead allowed to continue in its clearly imperfect form for another two centuries.

In 1806, Islanders obtained an Act of Parliament which partially converted the Knighten Court into a Court of Requests – dealing with debts of up to £5 – but left it nominally in existence. For a further four

This postcard from the 1907 Isle of Wight Pageant depicts a typical Island militiaman of the eighteenth century. It is particularly interesting for including in its top right-hand corner what appears to be the three-towered castle insignia of the Knighten Court.

decades, the two Courts existed side by side in Newport. Then, in 1847, both were swept away when, after the passing of another Act of Parliament, their jurisdiction was transferred to the new County Court. So ended this virtual 800-year legacy of FitzOsbern's feudal rule in the Isle of Wight.

THE ISLAND'S COURTS LEET

Once an integral part of administration in towns throughout England, the Court Leet was entrusted with many of the tasks principally carried out today by the trading standards and environmental health departments of the local authorities. In several towns, the Court also performed additional functions specific to the locality. While, remarkably, a few of the ancient Courts Leet survive to this day on the mainland – albeit with most of their original powers considerably diluted – those which once exercised control in Isle of Wight towns have long since disappeared.

In Newport, as befits the Island's capital, the Court Leet had 15 jurymen and a list of officers headed by the two chief constables. There were eight petty constables, a searcher of leather, two viewers of the butchers' shambles, two viewers of the 'gashing of hydes', two viewers of the Corn Market, two viewers of the Cheese Cross, eight measurers, a 'gager', two water bailiffs, a 'piggard', a 'pounder' and a 'whipper'. Each reported annually on any irregularities within their respective spheres of responsibility – short weights, uneven scales, dubious liquid measures and the like – and the jury would then sit in judgment and impose fines on the culprits.

Just as the pounder had the job of rounding-up straying cattle for the pound (and tending to their needs while they were in there), so the piggard kept his eyes open for errant porkers! Pigs were permitted a certain amount of freedom in the town, but it was a trip to the pound at the hands of the piggard – sometimes called the pig-driver – for any that became a nuisance. Local historian, R. J. Eldridge's research revealed the piggard's job as one to be avoided if at all possible. 'From reports made to the Court, it seems that he was frequently obstructed in his duty, insulted, and even assaulted,' wrote Eldridge in 1952. In 1748 the piggard of the day was consigned to the stocks because he had not properly carried out his duties. He also lost the job.

Unusually, there was a second Court Leet in Newport, which existed well into the nineteenth century. This dealt exclusively with matters pertaining to Castlehold, an area of land at the divergence of High Street and Pyle Street. Castlehold originally enclosed the 13 ½ building plots – or 'places', as they were known – retained for the use of the Lord of the Island at Carisbrooke Castle by the governing De Redvers family

Perhaps the most obvious relic of the days when Courts Leet were active on the Isle of Wight is the still-intact pound in Wall Lane, Brading.

late in the thirteenth century, when the freehold of the remainder of Newport was vested in the burgesses of the town. This meant that Castlehold was outside the jurisdiction of the town and its bailiffs, requiring its own Court Leet. By the nineteenth century, while the Town Clerk served as Judge to the Court Leet in Newport itself, Castlehold's jury was presided over by the Steward, or his deputy, of the Island's Governor.

Although the tasks entrusted to officers were much the same for most Courts Leet on the Island, there were local variations. In Brading, for example, the list of officers early in the seventeenth century reflected the status of the town (prior to the reclamation of Brading Haven) as a commercial port. Alongside the piggard, pounder, whipper, register of leather, several measurers, viewers of the various town markets and other common officials, was a keeper of the quay and fish shambles.

Yarmouth's Court Leet will forever be associated with the loss on 18 October 1784 of the Town Chest – together with the minute books, proceedings of the town's Corporation and historical documents, dating back centuries, which it contained. As was customary when the Court

[87]

Leet was in session, the oak chest had been taken from the Town Hall to the George Inn to receive the presentments of the Jury during the Court Leet Dinner, which was held at the George. Dining as a special guest of the Corporation on that particular evening was a naval officer, Lieutenant Charles Cunningham Crooke, whose ship, HMS *Expedition*, was lying in Yarmouth Road. Crooke, as it turned out, was aptly named.

The officer may have had too much to drink (or maybe, as some have suggested, he was aggrieved at having had too little) but at some stage of the evening he took his leave of the, no doubt, merry party – and the chest went with him. It was apparently some time before either was missed. By then HMS *Expedition* had weighed anchor and left the port. It is usually suggested that Crooke thought the chest contained the remainder of the evening's wine stock. Whatever his motives, it is probably safe to conclude that Crooke's discovery, when he opened the chest out at sea, of nothing more exciting (or valuable) inside than documents came as a great disappointment. For it is said that he promptly tossed Yarmouth's Town Chest and its irreplaceable municipal records overboard!

Incensed, the Corporation sued for £10,000 damages and was probably a trifle disappointed to be awarded only £500 by a jury at Winchester in July 1787. The Town Chest was never recovered. If you accept an alternative version of the legendary story, Crooke did eventually admit that he had removed the chest, and taken it to London to have the contents examined. However, the porter to whom its safe keeping was entrusted was robbed of both chest and papers. Crooke offered 20 guineas as a reward for their return, but did not succeed in retrieving his booty.

No further acts of infamy appear to have befallen the Court Leet at Yarmouth for the remainder of its existence, which was concluded in 1863 when the Mayor and Corporation agreed with the Town Clerk that its activities, 'especially with reference to the assize of bread and beer, and the inspection of weights and measures, and the appointment of constables, and the abatement of nuisance,' were obsolete. The Court Leet was suspended until further notice, and the Corporation in Yarmouth, declared a 'rotten borough' in 1880, was itself wound up in 1891.

COCK AND BULL STORIES

The Isle of Wight bears ample silent testimony to the suffering inflicted on animals by earlier generations in the name of public entertainment. The rebuilt Fighting Cocks Inn – recently restyled as a 'roadhouse' – at Hale Common, on the Sandown-Newport road, is an obvious example, but nowhere is the barbarism of the past so dramatically evoked that in the centre of Brading – the Bull Ring. There are, of course 'bull rings' in many other towns and cities – Birmingham's famous example springs immediately to mind – but they survive in name only. In Brading, the name is perpetuated along with the ring that was actually used to bait tethered bulls.

Moved in recent years the few yards from its traditional position – latterly on a pedestrian crossing island in the middle of the road – the heavy cast iron ring is now re-located in a less hazardous spot outside the 'new' Town Hall, by the High Street-West Street junction. It remains an attraction – but those who gather round it today are no longer baying for blood. Bull-baiting has been prohibited since 1835.

It had been a widespread and common practice for centuries, particularly during the Elizabethan era, and not merely for the recreation it provided for townspeople. Encouraging dogs – usually mastiffs – to repeatedly goad the tethered bull to tormented distraction was widely believed to improve the flavour of the meat following slaughter. Indeed, to slaughter a bull which had not been previously baited was a criminal offence! William Smith fell foul of the law at Brading in 1592 when the town authorities fined him sixpence for killing an unbaited beast. Selling unbaited meat was also punishable by law – and here the fine was considerably more severe. Another entry in Brading's town records reveals how local butcher William Waldron had no chance of a merry Christmas in 1593 when he was convicted of the crime during the festive season. His fine was a hefty 6s 8d (about 34p) – which probably eliminated a full week's takings at a stroke.

Once a year, bull-baiting at Brading acquired a festive spirit of its own. Sir John Oglander's sixteenth century diaries record how it was the custom 'from time immemorial' for the Governor of the Isle of Wight to give five guineas for the purchase of a bull for baiting which, following slaughter, would be distributed among the poor. The Mayor and Corporation attended the bullring in full ceremonial regalia,

From an Edwardian view of Brading showing (foreground) the bull ring in its
original position. It has since been removed away from the road for
preservation outside the 'new' Town Hall, though the area shown in the
picture is still referred to as Brading Bull Ring.

complete with mace-bearers and constables. Following a proclamation, the first dog – called 'the Mayor's dog' and ornamented with ribbons – was set upon the bull. Confusingly, this custom is sometimes linked not with Brading, but with Newport, and different sums of money are mentioned.

Evidence on the Newport link is somewhat confused, but there is no doubt bull-baiting was carried on elsewhere in the Island – though not always with legal sanction. Local laws governed when and where baiting could take place. It wasn't permitted, for example, at West Cowes in 1815, when George Bead was prosecuted for breaking the law in this regard. Baiting was allowed, however, five years later in Sandown – 15 years before its total prohibition – when Jonathan Williams returned home triumphantly to Brading, his home town, bearing the colours awarded by judges for setting the 'best dog' on the bull – confirmation that, at the time of its banishment, bull-baiting was established as a competitive sport.

Cock-fighting first found favour with the Romans but was much later adopted as an English – and Isle of Wight – custom. It was outlawed at the same time as the ban on bull-baiting, having generated much moral hostility towards the end of the eighteenth century. This was only partly due to growing national concern for the suffering of animals. Those who sought society's reform considered cock-fighting – along with the other blood sports enjoyed by the lower classes – an unsuitably brutish recreation which did nothing to aid the moral welfare of those who took part. The fact that cock-fighting encouraged gambling among the 'masses' was a particular bone of contention for the would-be reformers.

Possibly, this moral outrage was the reason for keeping secret the precise venue for a cock-fight on the Isle of Wight when the following notice was privately circulated in the town:

'Whit Monday, 1790. A main of cocks to fite for three guinneys prize, the second best cock to have a hat for a faver, and 8 cocks only; and naythur cock to be over four pouns and a half; to fite in the Parish of Northwood and to meet at 10 o'clock and hosever is a mind to put in a cock must give their names to John Dore and put down half a crown.'

A 'main' was the cock-fighter's term for a battle. The eight birds would be pitted against each other in a fight to the death until just four were left. The next stage would eliminate a further two and the surviving pair would then battle it out for the big prize. The 'hat for a faver' awarded to the second-best cock in the final entitled the owner to the proceeds of a hat passed among the spectators for whatever donation – or favour – they felt was appropriate. The bird, of course, would never fight again.

It should not, however, be thought that this cruel custom was the sole province of the lower classes. That was certainly not the case on the Isle of Wight, where the most celebrated breeder of fighting cocks was the Squire of Wackland, William Thatcher. The Squire – whose appetite for blood sports apparently knew no bounds – is said to have kept 50 game cocks at Wackland, just north of today's Fighting Cocks Cross. Spurred birds were set to fight to the death in a purpose-built cockpit at Wackland, roared on by an invited crowd, growing richer or poorer with every bout and bet. No doubt, many of the local birds selected to compete in the 'All England' championships at Westminster were trained here.

Happily, the only cock-fight to be seen on the Island now is the static re-enactment at Brading's wax museum.

RENYARD ON THE WIGHT

The Isle of Wight once happily boasted of having 'no hooded priests, no lawyers, no wolves and no foxes.' The origins of this have been traced back to the Tudor period. Dom Frederick Hockey's studious research into the medieval history of Wight suggests that the saying is derived from Paul Joviius, in his *Descriptio Britannica*, published in 1548. Since that was two years after Henry VIII's Dissolution of the Monasteries, the reference to the absence of 'hooded priests' needs little explanation. The wolf, ruthlessly persecuted throughout Britain, and probably extinct in England by the Elizabethan era, had almost certainly disappeared from the Isle of Wight by the mid-sixteenth century. Which leaves the lawyers and the foxes.

It wasn't until the mid-ninteenth century that Renyard (the 'y' and 'n' of the more usual Reynard were transposed in local dialect) was introduced to the Wight specifically for the chase. However, if local tradition is to be believed, it was the fondness of a clergyman for the fox – as a pet rather than a quarry – which led to the arrival of the first member of the species on the Island . . . and to the first fox hunt.

We don't know from where Parson Fenwick obtained his pet animal, but we are told he kept it in a kennel at Brook, on the Island's south-west coast. In 1830 the fox escaped. Evading capture, he caused havoc, raiding chicken houses and lambing pens. Finally, Squire Thatcher, Master of the Crockford Harriers, loaned his hounds for the pursuit of the Island's solitary fox. During Christmas week the pack's lack of experience at hunting anything but hares was put to the test when the Parson's erstwhile pet was spotted by a farmer cutting gorse on Brook Down. The fox ran gamely for a full 15 miles, but the hounds ran him to ground at Dungewood.

The story of the unfortunate animal's demise is told in a dialect ballad, one of the *Legends and Lays of the Isle of Wight* collected by the local writer Percy Stone for publication in 1912. This particular lay runs to no less than 28 stanzas, opening with:

> Passon Fenwick o' Brook a kep' a darg vox
> On a chain i' his yard at the rear;
> Where a got en, an' how, I niver yet heerd,
> All that I knows – he was theer.

From this we learn that the Parson's pet was a dog fox ('darg vox'). From the final verse – which breaks the form of the previous 27 and is not written in dialect – we learn that Squire Thatcher was the toast of the hunting fraternity at the conclusion of the chase:

> Charge your glasses – no 'heel taps' we make it our toast
> In the health I'm proposing tonight;
> Squire Thatcher of Wackland, I give as the toast
> Who ran the first fox in the Wight.

Squire Thatcher was flushed with success. Literally flushed, it seems. He got ridiculously drunk at a party to celebrate the death of Fenwick's fox and is said to have spent much of the evening 'entertaining' his companions by screaming at the top of his voice: 'I killed the fox! I killed the fox!' For the remaining 15 years of his life, the Wackland Squire bore the epithet 'The Fox Slayer' with considerable self-inflated pride. Throughout that period, however, he vociferously opposed the introduction of foxes to the Island, and a pack of hounds to hunt them – jealously guarding the status of the Crockford Harriers as the only organised hunt and, no doubt, his own 'fox slaying' uniqueness.

Thatcher's son, William, had no such reservations. He is credited by some sources (the other main contender is Benjamin Cotton, of Afton, Freshwater) with ferrying foxes across to the Island in 1845 – the year of the Squire's death – expressly for the hunt. They were apparently brought to Wackland and let out at nearby Newchurch. Some accounts refer to eight foxes. This is decreased to just a single pair in another of Percy Stone's collected lays, which suggests young Thatcher was accompanied on his fox-smuggling expedition:

> Me and him took to Portsmouth a trip -
> As a zay'd 'to gi' William a treat' -
> Brought your brace o' cubs home by zhip,
> An' nigh lost 'em in Union Street.

The reference to Union Street – which links upper and lower Ryde – indicates the foxes arrived at Ryde Pier, having crossed on the regular packet service from Portsmouth. The song may divert from the facts when it goes on to relate how, after being released at Wackland, the foxes later find themselves the quarry of the Harriers – led by an unsuspecting Squire Thatcher, who thinks he is in pursuit of 'ztoutish (stoutish) hares'. The foxes lead the hunt through Horringford Leaze . . .

> Me an' Squire, us hrode zide by zide;
> As us crossed by the wold 'Fightin' Cocks,'

Squire stood on his stirrups an' cried,
D-nation! they'm hrunning a vox!

In the song, the foxes outwit their pursuers – and in fact as well, it seems. By 1856, according to the writer W. H. Davenport Adams, the fox was 'as firmly established as the oldest inhabitant . . .' That remains the case today, with Renyard common in all parts of the Island, and particularly on rough ground such as The Undercliff – over which the present Isle of Wight Hunt exercises no control.

By 1845 there was apparently no shortage of lawyers, either. Another verse of the song recalling the arrival of the fox records the composition of the hunting party:

How a' mind they hrode for'ard and well,
Smith o' Languard an' Jacobs o' Chale.
Gibbs of Bowcombe an' Hills , too, o' Hale,
Grimes o' Yafford an' Day an' Scovell.
Hughes o' Whitcombe, Lord Alec the swell,
An' the lawyer chap, young Beckinsale.

ANIMAL TALES AND TRADITIONS

Of all the animals introduced to the Wight it was the rabbit which undoubtedly made the biggest impact – more so in the Island than on the mainland – and the animal crops up time and again in both historical studies and traditions.

The absence of the fox for so many centuries ensured a rapid and unchecked growth in the local rabbit population. As with the remainder of Britain, the 'coney,' as the animal was once commonly known – the term 'rabbit' was originally reserved for the young of the species – was introduced to the Isle of Wight following the Norman Conquest. The first, shipped across the Solent in the twelfth century, were restricted initially to walled enclosures before their – probably unintentional – release into the wild. Their subsequent expansion, free from the threat of the fox, was welcomed by the human population, for rabbits were an obvious and plentiful source of fresh food, while their skins were widely and variously used.

The species was so plentiful on the Isle of Wight that it was worth making the often awkward trip from the mainland – where the fox restricted the rabbit population – to share in this abundant offshore commodity. A story is told of frequent journeys made to the Island by a trader whose cross-Solent trips to buy local rabbits for the London markets earned him the nickname, the 'Coneyman'. Regular travel between the nation's capital and Wight was rare at the time and the Coneyman's trips assumed real importance when he took on the added role of postman, delivering letters from the Island's gentry to a London post-house.

Some of the methods used to catch rabbits on the Island were cruelly ingenious. An extraordinary method of ferreting for them was once employed by fishermen at Bembridge. No ferrets were actually used . . . just a crab with a candle! The candle's end was fixed to the back of a common king crab and then lit. Thus illuminated, the no doubt bewildered crustacean was thrust, by means of a long stick, as far as possible into a rabbit burrow. It was then urged to penetrate even deeper by the gentle pulling by the fisherman of a string attached to one of its legs. Alarmed at the sight of the approaching light, the unfortunate

The Island's plentiful supply of rabbits (coneys) have helped to keep
its inhabitants well-fed for centuries. This drawing is of the 'coneyman'
who visited the Island to take rabbits for the London markets, and doubled
up as a postman!

An undated view of the Hare and Hounds pub at Downend, which remains a favourite hostelry for Islanders.

rabbit would bolt for an alternative entrance to the burrow – straight into the fisherman's net.

The brown hare is generally regarded as a native – as opposed to an introduced – species, but its numbers on the Island have been artificially boosted on occasions. Re-stocking on a large scale was required in the sixteenth century. 'We had infinite of coneys but not one hare,' wrote the diarist Sir John Oglander of the period leading up to 1574, the year Sir Edward Horsey, Captain of the Isle of Wight, rectified the situation with an unusual exchange deal: a lamb for a hare. Concerned at the lack of hares for coursing, the influential Sir Edward persuaded many of his mainland friends to help stock the Island with the missing rodent. This did not prove too much of a difficulty once he had tempted them with the offer of a lamb for every live hare brought in. In no time, a good many hares were shipped across until the Island, as Sir John Oglander put it, was sufficiently 'stored'.

Unlike its badgers – introduced to the Isle of Wight at about the same time as the fox, deemed extinct early this century, re-introduced in 1925, and now happily re-established – the Island has never replaced its deer stocks, which last roamed wild on Wight up to 200 years ago. As with the fox and the hare, red and fallow deer were brought across the Solent expressly for the chase; the medieval hunting grounds of

Parkhurst and Borthwood were well stocked with both species. Wild deer, however, remained a common enough sight on the Isle of Wight even after the last of the wild herds had disappeared! For 'deer' was one of the Islanders' optional words for *agrositis setacea* or Bristle Bent. It was also called, with a greater degree of descriptive element, Deer's Foot Grass or Rabbit Grass.

There is one other animal which, from time to time in the Isle of Wight, is still hotly pursued by man. The Island's broad-leaved woodlands are one of the last remaining strongholds in the South for Britain's native red squirrel. It used to be said that a squirrel could travel from one end of the Island to the other without touching the ground. This delightful creature was once so plentiful that squirrel hunts were organised on Wight – and squirrel pie was a local delicacy. But these days, it is not the 'reds' which are hunted on the Island. When the North American grey squirrel, which has ousted the 'red' from so much of its mainland habitat, very occasionally strays onto a cross-Solent ferry – usually the western route from Lymington, the mainland port adjacent

Recalling the chase – the inn sign at the Hare and Hounds.

[99]

to the New Forest – he finds a less than cheery welcome on arrival in Wight . . . and the quickest of day returns!

However, when it comes to unwanted visits from members of the animal kingdom, it is birds that Islanders fear – or used to fear – the most. Specific species of birds have down the centuries been the subject of a host of local superstitions. A robin pecking at the window was once believed to foretell a death in the family. Whether magpies flew to the right or the left, and how many there were of them, was considered a strong indicator of good or bad luck; happy or disastrous events. Most feared of all were the ravens. Their presence near dwellings was considered to presage death – and there was plenty of evidence to support this.

It was thought – and probably still is in some quarters – that a raven's strong sense of smell attracts the bird to a deceased person. 'My sister-in-law told me that previous to the death (from fever) of one of her children at Landguard (just to the west of Shanklin), two ravens sat daily in the lime tree near the house, and did not leave until the child was buried,' recalled C. Roach Smith in an appendix to the glossary of Isle of Wight words he edited for the English Dialect Society in 1881.

Down the ages, Islanders may have hunted the animals – but they have been haunted by the birds.

A TRIP TO THE FAIR

I bunched a tutty big ez a plate
an' garbed me up a dandy-o.
To meet my maayde by her mammy's gate
an' away to Newtown Randy O.

When expressed as a noun rather than its more common adjectival use, the word 'randy' refers to a country fair or revel. This may produce a feeling of let-down among some of the less informed visitors who make their way to the Newtown Randy in August with certain expectations. However, for those who appreciate the continuance – or in this case revival – of medieval local traditions, out-of-the-way Newtown's summer fair is a delightful reminder of former importance. A 'tutty', incidentally, is local dialect for a nosegay or bunch of flowers.

As with their markets, medieval towns were granted the right to hold fairs under the terms of their charter. The boisterous activity of the annual fair was eagerly anticipated by the ordinary townsfolk, for whom it provided a rare chance to escape the daily drudgery of working life. Making merry – in every sense of the phrase – was the order of the day. Fairs were usually organised to coincide with the feast day of the saint to whom the local church was dedicated, and they often lasted for several days. Some towns held more than one – on the Isle of Wight, Brading celebrated in both May and October – but few survive today. The Island, however, provides noteworthy exceptions to the general rule of decline.

Most ancient of the Island's medieval boroughs, Newtown enjoyed municipal privileges which probably pre-dated the Norman Conquest, and were first granted when the town was known by its former name of Francheville. Whether this once thriving sea port held an annual fair prior to the fourteenth century is a matter for conjecture, but it certainly had the right to do so from 1318 onwards. In that year Edward II's charter confirmed certain privileges which included a weekly market and an annual three-day fair 'on the eve, the day and the morrow of the Feast of St. Mary Magdalene,' to whom the town's first chapel had been dedicated.

The highly-valued right to hold a fair reflected the considerable importance of the place at this time – but it was a status soon to be savagely removed by the devastating French attack of 1377. There must have been a lengthy period of inactivity in the years that followed, but the fair was eventually revived and was then held annually up until 1781, despite the vastly reduced fortunes of a town which had only been partially rebuilt. A further brief revival took place in 1920, in aid of Newtown's church. Half-a-century later, in 1973, Porchfield and Newtown's Women's Institute, in need of funds towards hall maintenance costs, re-launched the Randy. The fair has happily remained an annual event – albeit now held in August – ever since.

Nearby Yarmouth may well have been unique in celebrating 25 July, St. James's Day, as the date for its annual fair – or the date which fell in the middle of a series of fair days. The reason was simple enough since one of Yarmouth's two long-vanished eleventh century churches was dedicated to St. James the Apostle and Martyr – a dedication also chosen for the present church, completed in 1626. Probably first held in the sixteenth century, under the terms of a charter granted to the town by James I, the St. James's Day Fair (or Fayre) is still celebrated in Yarmouth following a recent revival – complete with observance of its principal custom.

The fair was the one time of the year the townsfolk could get away, if not exactly with murder, than at least with a host of lesser crimes. This relaxation of the long arm of the law, the 'open hand' to do just about anything you wanted without fear of incurring too strict a penalty, was signified by the display of a stuffed glove on the end of a pole protruding from the first floor of the Town Hall in The Square. While the hand remained open, overindulgence was the accepted order of the day. The custom of the open hand (which also seems to have been observed at Newchurch village's May Fair) is still exercised annually on the nearest Sunday to St. James's Day. Overindulgence is usually pursued in the local hostelries.

Newport's long-established Whitsuntide Fair had run into serious problems by the mid-nineteenth century. 'The annual fair is held on Whit Monday, and two succeeding days, but it exhibits a mere shadow of its once pristine splendour,' wrote W. H. Davenport Adams in his *History, Topography and Antiquities of the Isle of Wight*, published in 1856. That was one way of putting it.

Since the fair was held principally in the Corn Market (later St. Thomas' Square) and centred on a pavilion outside the market building itself, the festivities were directly opposite the main doors of St. Thomas' Church. It provoked so much ill-feeling that, in 1845, the Corporation was presented with a petition, signed by a good number of Newport's inhabitants, deploring the annual outbreak of 'drunkenness

The Square at Yarmouth, where a gloved hand traditionally emerged from the first floor of the Town Hall, denoting relaxation of the law during fair-time.

and debauchery' so near to the town's principal place of worship, and asking that the fair, if it could not be stopped altogether, should be moved to another site. This led to regulations which, as far as possible, confined the fair to the Beast Market (now St. James's Square) and Quay Street.

Moved on they may have been, but the Whitsuntide revellers were singularly unmoved by the righteous indignation their less than restrained activities continued to engender in the town. In 1858 matters finally came to a head. Clergy, Sunday School teachers and a good many others united in common prayer and complaint as they mounted a concerted effort to put an end to the Whitsuntide Fair once and for all. Bombarded with representations about the general immorality of the event and the fascination it undoubtedly held for 'undesirables' from many other parts of the Island, the Corporation bowed to the pressure.

Stallholders' tolls and fees were deliberately raised to such high levels that it was all but impossible for the fair to continue. Having delivered this body blow, the Corporation then killed off the fair altogether with new powers given to it under the Fairs Act. All this was happily forgotten in 1996 when the Michaelmas tradition was resurrected in Newport town centre, stallholders wearing button holes of Michaelmas daisies as the revived fair raised money for a children's charity.

NIPPERT'S BARGAN ZATTERDAYS

People no doubt still go looking for bargains in Newport's bustling town centre on a Saturday shopping trip. They are, however, unlikely to snap up the sort of bargains that, well into the nineteenth century, were annually negotiated in the Island's capital on the three weekends leading up to Old Michaelmas Day on 11 October. The deals struck at Newport's Bargain Saturdays were concerned with just two commodities – men and women! On those three days the town centre filled with earnest young farm servants hoping to catch the eye and secure a further year's work.

While 'hiring fairs' at Michaelmas were not uncommon on the mainland, Newport's appear to have been the only such events held on the Island, as befitted the town's size, central location and capital status. The three hiring days – known colloquially in 'Nippert' as Vust (First), Middle and Last Bargan Zatterdays – would see the men gather at the Beast Market in St. James's Square and the women in the High Street at Gape Mouth Corner, opposite the Vine Inn. Dressed always in their best clothes, they came from all parts of the Isle to strike a bargain with the farmers.

For one of the best descriptions of Bargain Saturdays, we are indebted to the fascinating early nineteenth century memoirs of Mark William Norman (published by Ventnor & District Local History Society in 1988), who recorded that 'the young men mostly wore blue, short sailor's jackets, with rows of buttons each side, a coloured or black neckerchief, a cotton shirt with blue stripes and high collar, sometimes a red waistcoat with black spots and pearl buttons, drab corduroy trousers, and a light pair of homemade lace-up boots, a broad-brimmed hat and a bandana handkerchief in the jacket. The lasses were addicted to ribbons, lace and bright coloured cotton prints, some with waist ribbands, and low shoes. The townspeople called them Jans and Marys.'

There was, however, rather more to a Bargain Saturday than the bargaining itself, for they were also regarded by the farm servants as their annual fête days. Once the formalities of hiring the workforce were completed, many of the young folk turned their attentions to the

'Jans and Mary's' bargain with prospective employers at the annual 'Bargan Zatterdays' hiring fair in Newport.

business of drinking, dancing and general merry-making. Large dancing rooms at several of the town's pubs, such as the Red Lion, the Lamb and, especially, the Bell Chamber, were packed solid as the country visitors raucously rounded-off their day in town. It was usually the case that Bargain Saturdays degenerated into a general free-for-all of loud arguments and brawls, with rivals for the title of 'best man' adjourning to the open air of Trattle's Butt to settle the score with their fists.

Mark Norman vividly recalled that 'the dances were four or six hand reels, noted more for the noise of stamping on the floor than for (keeping) time to the music, played by a fiddler – some shoemaker or tailor, who had devoted his leisure hours to the study of the violin. There is no accounting for tastes. Else how could they bear the crush, the dust, the smell of bad tobacco, and the perspiration teeming off them at every pore? Refreshments were mostly spirits and water – 'sixpenny worth of red stuff in a beason' – served in a small earthenware basin holding about half-a-pint, because so many glasses could be broken, as were the basins also in quarrelling and fighting.'

Annual rituals connected with the work of local people – particularly those associated with the food crops of land and sea – were also organised in other areas of the Island. A Crab Fair is still arranged each year at Ventnor, a revival of a two-day event held outside the Crab and Lobster Inn on 7-8 May until 1846, and nearby Niton still holds its Mackerel Fair in June – a throwback to the days when the winding-up of the local mackerel fishing season was celebrated by Midsummer Day merry-making. 'Mackerel midge,' as the locals called them, were fished in Chale Bay, between Atherfield and Blackgang Chine. Writing in 1781, Sir Richard Worsley described Niton's midsummer fair as taking place in the area of the maypole near the Star Inn, adding that the round of festivities ended with a ball in the White Lion Inn.

Early in the nineteenth century, Mark Norman recalled 'a few gingerbread stalls, each presided over by an old dame, near the Star hostelry,' and said the evening's ball was 'usually attended by the lads and lasses of the village and neighbourhood, and by some of the middle-aged paters and maters.' The music, he added, 'was discoursed on an ancient fiddle by a then old fisherman, bronzed by exposure, with hands of horn and big with all that; the wonder was how he managed to finger the strings. However, he accomplished it so well as to give general satisfaction, and had occupied the post during many years both at midsummer and at Christmas, when another dance took place in the evening of Boxing Day.' Prolonged to a late hour, the dances, 'of those so called country,' were rounded-off by the 'Sir Roger de Coverley' or 'Thread-the-Needle' dance.

The harvesting of the sea crop has always been synonymous with Niton, which formerly held a twice-weekly fish market at the Village Cross, and used to be commonly referred to as Crab-Niton to distinguish it from the hamlet of Knighton (still pronounced locally as K-nighton) near Newchurch. Worsley logically suggested the name Crab-Niton was used because of the 'plenty of sea crabs on that coast.' This, one assumes, is the preferred option in the village today ... the alternative is that it was so-named because the inhabitants were crabbed and ill-natured!

ENGLAND'S FIRST
CARNIVAL

The now traditional English street carnival celebrated its centenary in 1988 . . . at Ryde. There seems little doubt that the Isle of Wight town was truly, as it has always claimed to be, the birthplace of the 'modern' carnival in this country. There are rivals to the title, but Ryde is able to prove that its inaugural carnival was held in 1888 – and was almost certainly the first to be so termed.

In fact, Ryde had organised what amounted to a carnival procession in just about everything but name in 1887, the Golden Jubilee of Queen Victoria's accession to the throne. The Queen left Osborne House, her beloved Isle of Wight home at East Cowes, on 28 July that year to pay a special Jubilee visit to Ryde. A major part of the celebrations to mark the occasion was a torchlight procession through the streets of the town, although it appears to have been held after the Queen herself had returned to Osborne. According to contemporary newspaper reports, the procession featured the town's Volunteer Band, the Fire Brigade, and a host of townsmen dressed in fancy costume and bearing torches.

'Such a stirring procession has never been seen before at Ryde,' enthused the *Isle of Wight Observer*, which was soon reporting on the town's determination to hold another procession in 1888 as an event in its own right. Organised along similar lines to the Jubilee parade, but on a larger scale, the 1888 event was the brainchild of William Gibbs (whose Gibbs & Gurnell chemists' shop remains a distinctive feature of Ryde's Union Street to this day) and Gustav Mullins, who ran the Hughes & Mullins photographic business in the town. To these two men – Gibbs as Chairman and Treasurer; Mullins as Joint Secretary with John Parnell, who had organised the 1887 procession – belongs the credit for devising almost certainly the first-ever carnival in England.

'Carnival' was the name given to the season immediately before Lent, which was celebrated in some Roman Catholic countries by processions, dancing, feasting and general merry-making. Ryde's decision to adopt this particular title for its procession in 1888 seems to have had few, if any, precedents elsewhere in England. According to the *Observer*, Gibbs and Mullins 'thought that by calling the affair a Carnival they might induce a larger number of the general public to join in the fun.' On the evening of Friday, 17 August the first Ryde Grand Carnival and Torchlight Procession set off from Lind Street, opposite the Town Hall. 'A lengthy and very pretty procession,' thought the *Observer*.

Indeed, the parade was so lengthy that Lind Street could hold barely half of it and the scheduled 8pm start was delayed by half-an-hour. However, the newspapers indicated less that wholehearted support from the townsfolk. 'Our cold northern temperament, perhaps, is responsible for that,' suggested the *Observer*. 'As a Frenchman once said of us, we have no equivalent for the word *s'amuse*; we always take our pleasures sadly. We must confess, therefore, there was not an exuberance of that boisterous spirit (always supposed to be associated with a carnival) amongst the thousands who crowded our streets last night.'

A gusty wind didn't help – difficulty was experienced keeping the Chinese lanterns and torches alight – but overall the *Observer* felt the event was 'a great success for the first attempt.' Twelve clowns preceded the Volunteer Band at the head of a parade which relied heavily on the theme of royalty for its characters. More than 30 English sovereigns were depicted, and there was a 'carefully arranged and very much admired tableau' of Victoria and her Colonies. Among others, the parade also featured Robin Hood and his men, an Arab chief, twelve 'ghosts'. Ryde Town Band, Morris dancers, several other tableaux and 100 local children with Chinese lanterns, tambourines and trumpets.

While many of the costumes appear to have been hired, there were flashes of the ingenuity and improvisation which is such a feature of carnival costume design today. 'Here and there,' reported the *Observer*, 'a figure was interpolated which seemed rather incongruous. For instance, there was a man in armour formed of tin pots, saucepan lids etc.!' He may well have thought it expedient to change into something rather more practical for the masquerade ball in the Town Hall which brought down the curtain on proceedings later that night. The first carnival cost £70 to mount and made a profit of £8 16s 11d (£8.85).

Ryde repeated the carnival in 1889 (with Queen Victoria among the spectators) and other Island towns were quick to follow its lead. The organisation of Ryde's event was sporadic in the early years, and there were later periods of inactivity (between 1906 and 1934, then during the Second World War), but the hard work and dedication of successive carnival committees has kept it going without further break since revival in 1949. Three processions are organised – a children's parade, the main procession and the ever-popular Saturday night illuminated procession, which traditionally brings down the curtain on the Isle of Wight's carnival season at the end of August. Ground events and a host

Town centre crowds await the arrival of Ryde's carnival procession -
traditionally led by the stirring sight of a mounted cavalier. That particular
tradition may be a thing of the past, but the Carnival itself continues to thrive,
celebrating its 110th anniversary in 1998.

of other attractions augment the processions in the modern carnival
week.

It's not only towns which stage carnivals. St. Helens had organised its
annual fair and sports on the village green since the early years of
the nineteenth century, originally to coincide with the November 5th
celebrations. By 1906, with festivities switched to the summer, a carnival
parade had been added. St. Helens Sports and Carnival is still with us
and has been an August Bank Holiday fixture since 1948 (and this
enterprising village still arranges one of the best Bonfire Night events,
too). Towns, villages, even housing estates, organise carnivals these
days and, despite ever-spiralling costs and competition from counter
attractions, they continue to draw the crowds. A summer without them
would be unthinkable.

HERE WE COME A SHROVEN

Shroven, Shroven,
I be come a Shroven.
A piece of bread, a piece of cheese,
A piece of your fat bacon.
Doughnuts and pancakes,
All o' your own maaken.
Vine vowls in a pie,
My mouth es very dry.
I wish I was zo well a-wet,
I'd zing the better vor a nut.
Shroven, Shroven,
We be come a Shroven.

Apart from the annual Hallowe'en ritual of trick-or-treat, an American import of fairly recent times, children no longer call at the front doors of their neighbours in town or village to mark specific days or festivals with time-honoured customs – usually involving a boisterous rendition of rhyme or song such as the one above.

'Shroven,' as this dialect word (a local corruption of the more usual 'shroving') implies, was a Shrove Tuesday custom. Once common throughout England, shroving – also known as 'gooding' – dates back several centuries and originated as a form of begging by the poor at a particularly difficult time of year. There was little to be had from the land in February and even the basic ingredients for a Shrove Tuesday pancake were beyond the pockets of many. So they were forced to beg for the traditional fare from their wealthier neighbours. Their appeals were not confined to the pancakes themselves – food in general and money were also sought – but eventually this annual expression of need developed into a more lighthearted country custom. Accompanied always by traditional verse, it was increasingly left to children, who eagerly anticipated the yearly ritual.

The young 'shrovers' would gather in the early morning, then go from house to house singing for their 'Shrove cakes' – or a variety of optional tasty snacks if cakes were in short supply. In practice, the houses they called at were usually those of the principal inhabitants only, beginning with the gentry and ending with the farmers. The song was an important part of the procedure; those who sang it the loudest were reckoned to be the best shrovers and were often rewarded with an extra cake or a penny for their effort. There were clearly several variations of the song in the Island – and elsewhere – but all of them shared the same basic elements.

The version above is that quoted by W. H. Long in *A Dictionary of the Isle of Wight Dialect* (1886). According to at least two other sources, a variation with a distinctively different opening verse was sung by the children of Newchurch village until the outbreak of the First World War:

> Shroven, Shroven,
> Here we come a-Shroven.
> A piece of bread, a piece of cheese,
> A piece of your fat bacon.
> The roads are very dirty,
> Our boots are very thin.
> We have a little pocket
> To put a penny in.

In Newchurch the song seems to have been initially performed at midday outside the post office and village shop. The baker, in his cap and apron, would appear after the children's rendition and throw a shower of 'goodies' in their midst. Then, having feasted, the shrovers would move off to repeat the ritual at the Vicarage and other large houses in the locality – no doubt until hunger was satisfied!

While no specific reference to it is made in any of the Isle of Wight versions of the 'shroven' song, it is quite probable that the allied custom of 'Lent crocking' was practiced here. Refusal to come up with the items requested by the shrovers meant a bombardment of the front door with broken pottery, stones and anything else that came to hand. Shades of the modern trick-or-treat! A suggested origin for this was the fact that, with Lent beginning the next day, cooking pots and the like were not going to be needed in the usual quantity until the fast was concluded. An optional explanation for the throwing of pottery shards at doors is simpler. It was good fun!

In common with the rest of the country, Islanders still toss pancakes and run races with the finished product on Shrove Tuesday, but the other traditions have disappeared – including the ancient, but much rarer, custom, observed in Newport, of 'ringing the bell' on Pancake Day. The bell in question was the sixth (the 'pan' bell) at St. Thomas' Church, which was rung at eleven in the morning on Shrove Tuesday as a prelude to the start of the Lenten fast the following day.

Pancake races, which in some areas of the country
date back to the fifteenth century, remain a popular
Shrove Tuesday custom on the Island.

Pancake bells were rung originally to release servants, labourers and
apprentices from their duties on Shrove Tuesday, allowing them to
join in the day's festivities.

IN THE MERRY MONTH
OF MAY

Although village schoolchildren still dance round the maypole to welcome the arrival of the 'merry month' on the Isle of Wight, and young girls are still crowned Queen of the May, many of the Island's Maytime traditions have long since disappeared.

Back in the sixteenth century – and probably for centuries before that – the people of Newport waited longer than most to celebrate May Day. In those days, it was customary for country folk to take to the woods on the eve of 1 May and spend the night collecting small branches of May blossom (hawthorn), returning as the sun rose to deck their homes and welcome the arrival of summer. A day filled with music and much merriment would follow. This delightful custom was energetically observed at Newport, but, for reasons obscured by time, always on the first Saturday night *after* May Day.

Contemporary accounts tell of the town bailiffs annually appointing a Lord to preside over the May festival. Colourfully dressed, he would usually have a Lady at his side, and would be served by a minstrel together with – a throw-back to the morality plays of the Middle Ages – a devilish character known as the 'vice', who adopted a witty, mischievous and profligate manner! On the Saturday, the Lord and his servants would ride through the town with, we are told, 'a pretie compayne of youths followinge them,' stopping at each house to order the townsfolk's attendance at nearby Parkhurst Forest in the early hours of the following morning to fetch home the May blossom. Anyone failing to make it to the forest before sunrise would be fined 'a green goose and a gallon of wyne.'

In the early hours of the morning, the bailiffs and town burgesses presented themselves at Parkhurst, where they were met by the forest keepers, who saluted their arrival and, in recognition of their status, symbolically offered each of them small green boughs. This ceremony over, it was the turn of 'ye commen people of ye towne', equipped with hatchets and other cutting tools, to enter the forest and remove their own flowering sprigs from the plentiful supply of May blossom. Placed later over the doors and round the windows of the houses in town, the sprigs would refresh the streets, giving 'a commodious and

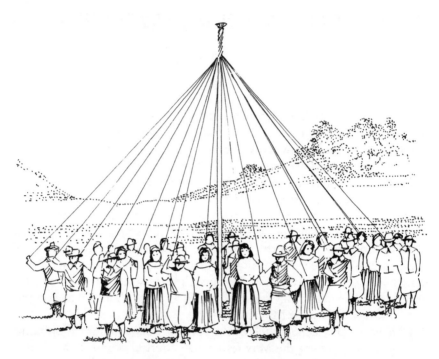

An Elizabethan Maypole dance on the Isle of Wight.

pleasant umbrage to ye houses and comfort to ye people passing bye.'

The highlight was the torchlit processional return from forest to town. A set order was observed, with the 'commoners' always at the head. Following them would be the forest keepers, the minstrel, the vice and a group of Morris dancers. Then came the town sergeants, complete with maces, followed by the bailiffs and burgesses (or co'burgs, as they were more generally known at the time). The company marched triumphantly to Newport's Corn Market where, 'after casting themselves off in a ringe', all except the co'burgs and forest keepers dispersed. Those remaining then sat down to a prepared breakfast. After that, the normal routine of a Sunday morning was observed with morning prayer – but the fun was far from over. In the evening, minstrels and dancers took to the streets as the town began a rather more boisterous celebration of the merry month of May.

Perhaps the most striking thing about the Maytime celebrations was its total involvement of Newport's population. Everyone, from those at the top of the social ladder to those at the bottom, went to

Parkhurst Forest for the pre-dawn cutting of the boughs. The fact that the Corporation took part helped to ensure that the celebrations did not stray unacceptably beyond the usual limits of good order – pubs were still in their infancy – and the objectives of this particular festival were universally held to be 'good companye, myrthe and honest pleasure.'

Despite this, the custom – in its fullest form – surprisingly seems to have died out in Newport before the arrival of the seventeenth century. It did, however, survive beyond that in an abbreviated style which saw a formal parade on 1 May by boys of the town – known as Jacks-in-the-Green – carrying the traditional boughs of small trees. When this, too, had been consigned to the pages of history, no serious attempt at revival was made until 1994. In that year, thanks to the intervention of the present-day forest keepers – the Forestry Commission – the May blossom tradition was back on the agenda. The cutting of hawthorn sprigs at Parkhurst Forest took place that year on Sunday, 1 May and was followed by a procession to the Wheatsheaf Hotel in Newport's St. Thomas' Square (the site of the former Corn Market) which was then decorated with the freshly-cut sprigs in traditional style.

Yarmouth's own 1 May custom was something of a variation on the Newport theme. Small girls – 'prettily dressed in light summer frocks,' according to one local historian – used to celebrate May Day by carrying garlands of wild flowers round the town. Stopping at virtually every front door, they would chant . . .

> Oh, the first of May is Garland Day.
> So please to remember the Garland, the Garland,
> Oh, please to remember the Garland . . .

and the request was almost always granted with the presentation of a fresh garland.

THE HOOAM HARVEST

No event in the rural calendar of Wight was celebrated more heartily than the 'bringing home' of a successful harvest. The prosperity of the farmer, all those who worked for him and their respective families was entirely dependent upon it.

Thus, the gathering-in of the final load from the fields was an event of tremendous significance. As such, it was usually attended by a considerable degree of ceremony. A 'puncheon' (small keg) of what Islanders called 'nammet beer' would often be drunk in the fields before the stately procession of the last waggon-load, topped with green boughs, into the 'rickess' (rickyard). While this was taking place, the farmer's wife, helped by her maids and probably a few of her neighbours, would be busy in the kitchen preparing a very special 'Harvest Home' supper. Islanders colloquially knew it as 'Hooam Harvest' – a great outpouring of relief and happiness presided over by the farmer but enjoyed by everyone on the farm.

Not surprisingly, in view of its importance to the collective welfare of the rural population, memories of the pre-mechanised Isle of Wight harvest have been well chronicled. Recalling ninteenth century custom in West Wight, Yarmouth historian A.G. Cole remembered the parish church always being crowded for the evening Harvest Thanksgiving service.

'After it was all over,' he wrote, 'the employees of the late James Blake would adjourn to the old mill for the Harvest Home Supper. There would be carters, dairymen, labourers, and men from the mills at Shalfleet and Yarmouth, with their womenfolk, and the ground floor of the mill, its walls gaily decorated with bunting, was filled to capacity. After grace had been said, and before the supper, there were two toasts – "the Queen" and "the Master" – the latter generally responded to by the host of the evening.'

The repast, added Cole in his memoirs, was always the same – 'huge joints of roast beef, boiled hams, mashed potatoes, numerous other vegetables, plum pudding, treacle, cheese – and unlimited beer. Everyone thoroughly enjoyed themselves, singing old songs and having a few country dances as the evening wore on.'

A vastly more detailed account of 'Hooam Harvest' is provided by W. H. Long in his 1886 guide to the Isle of Wight's dialect and rural

Country folk celebrating bringing in the harvest.

traditions. Recording it firmly as 'a thing of the past', but a tradition which had been followed by the farming community in more or less the same way since 'time immemorial', Long says it had been observed mostly by the smaller farms, cultivating 100 or 200 acres, who kept the majority of their men 'in house' and supplied them with meat and drink throughout the demanding harvest period. With the wheat and barley cut for the day, an evening would end after supper with songs and an extra pint or two of strong beer – a kind of rehearsal for the real 'Hooam Harvest' to come.

Labourers and 'extra men,' adds Long, were fed and watered on the same terms as the farmer's yearly servants, engaged from Michaelmas to Michaelmas and all were invited to the huge supper which crowned and concluded the harvest – as were the carpenter and blacksmith who, along with their apprentices, willingly gave their time to help out on the busiest days of the 'harvest month'. No doubt, all would have been present when that last load was ceremonially unpitched in the 'rickess' and relaxation was at last the order of the day.

'In a very short space of time,' Long's narrative continues, 'the carters, farm servants and labourers, with faces glowing with expectations and ruddy from a recent swill, arranged themselves round a long table; "Meyester" (the Master) and his select circle, the carpenter and blacksmith generally included, being seated at a cross table at the top of the other, or, if crowded, at a separate board, as near the labourers' table as convenient.

'A large leg of mutton, a ham to match, or sometimes two, with mutton pies, or a chine, constituted the first course, followed by plum puddings of huge dimensions, sometimes accompanied by an apple pie of even larger diameter. "Meyester" generally carved at the top of the table and one of the invited guests, at the bottom.'

With plates considerably lightened, and the tables cleared, jugs of 'Hooam Harvest Stingo' were placed before the men, together with pipes and tobacco, while the farmer and his party were served bottles of spirits 'and the necessary ingredients for making grog' along with their own smoking requisites. Then the fun really began. One of the men would be called upon for a song and considerable good-humoured banter would follow as he protested that he 'never was noo zinger.' Eventually, adds Long, 'after a few vigorous "hems" and a deep draught of ale, he commences in a tone in which strength makes up for want of harmony':

> As I walked out one Maay mornen,
> One Maay mornen so early,
> I overtook a handsome maade,
> Just as the zun was a risen.
> Wi' my rum tum ta,
> And my rum tum ta,
> Fol lol the diddle lol the dido.

However, the most commonly recalled song from the 'Hooam Harvest' – and there was a veritable repertoire of them – was usually left for the oldest labourer to perform:

> Here's a health unto our meyester,
> The founder o' the feast.
> I hopes wi' all my heart, bwoys,
> His soul in heaven med rest.
> That all the things wull prosper,
> That ever he takes i hand,
> Vor we be all his servants,
> And all at his command.
> Then drink bwoys, drink, and zee you don't spill,
> Vor if you do, you shall drink two,
> If 'tis our meyester's will.

The next day, Long concludes, 'was always more or less a holiday.'

REMEMBERING THE FIFTH

The 'popish plot' origins of the most celebrated failure in English history are unlikely to figure prominently in the thoughts of children the length and breadth of the nation as, annually in November, they attempt, with varying degrees of endeavour and success, to produce a passable imitation of the ill-fated Guy Fawkes from all manner of discarded clothing, soft furnishings and other household items well past their 'use by' date. When they 'remember the Fifth of November', the original anti-Catholic sentiment behind this yearly commemoration is usually consumed in the unquenching thirst for fun and fireworks.

This was not the case a century or so ago on the Isle of Wight. Then, as now, having fun was still the order of the day, but the late-Victorian Bonfire Night rituals recalled much more of the venom that was originally directed against the Catholic plotters – and their papal inspiration. At least, they certainly did in Yarmouth.

Writing in 1948 of his boyhood years in the town, A.G. Cole provides us with a graphic depiction of November 5th in the west of the Island. It was, he recalls, 'perhaps the greatest day of the year in Yarmouth.' For weeks beforehand, local men and boys would collect 'bushes and wood' from the countryside to build a huge bonfire on what was then a broad strip of common land at the foot of the hill giving access to the town from Newport and the east of the Island.

'On the morning of "The Fifth" boys would carry round the town in an old chair hideous guys dressed in disreputable clothes, supposed to be in the fashion of 1605, and having in one hand an old lantern and, in the other, a box of lucifer matches. They stopped in front of nearly every door chanting an old anti-papal song:

> Oh, tis the Fifth of November
> And you'll please to remember
> The gunpowder, treason and plot.
> And the King does desire a good bonfire,
> And I hope it will not be forgot.
> Hip, hip hooray!
> Hip, hip hooray!
> Hip, hip hooray!
> We want a fathom of rope

To hang the Pope,
A faggot of wood to toast him;
A penn'orth of cheese to make him sneeze,
And a jolly good fire to roast him.

Three more cheers would follow, the householders would come to their doors and, after criticising the guys, would decide how many pence or half-pence should be given for the imaginary purchase of rope, faggots and cheese.'

The bonfire, however, would not be lit until the mail-cart ('a peculiar red-painted pillbox-like vehicle') had left the town, to avoid the blaze frightening the horse.

'As soon as this had passed and was a safe distance away, the pile of inflammable material was set on fire, the various guys thrown on it, and the male spectators amused themselves by hurling fire-balls through the air. These were made of finely-picked oakum, bound tightly into balls by strands of wire, with a stout wire handle. They had been soaked for some days in benzine, so made a big blaze when lit, and a loud, roaring noise when thrown through the air.'

Many of the elements described by Cole are recognisable today, though in somewhat modified form. Yarmouth's communal bonfire was taken off the calendar after 1893 following the tragic death of a male spectator, killed when the huge pile toppled over on top of him. Happily, in somewhat more controlled conditions, communal bonfires are still organised on the Island – notably at St. Helens, where the celebrations usually include a parade of 'guys' through the village.

No longer observed is another November tradition once celebrated annually by Isle of Wight blacksmiths on the 23rd – St. Clement's Day. Although St. Clement is the patron saint of tanners – his own trade – he was appropriated by the Island's blacksmiths, who marked 23 November in, literally, explosive fashion. In the evening they and their friends would set off squibs of powder on their anvils.

This odd custom was known as 'keeping up Clem' and is delightfully noted in W. H. Long's nineteenth century dialect dictionary: 'The blacksmiths be gwyne to keep up Clem to-morrow night, you; they've zended to Yarmouth vor a pound o' powder.' Having duly 'kept up' the memory of St. Clement, the blacksmiths would then adjourn to the local alehouse for what Long describes as 'songs and festivity'.

Edward Turner, writing at the turn of the century, suggests there was significance, over and above an excuse for a good night out, in the evening's finale. 'The symbol of St. Clement is a pot,' he wrote, 'because November 23rd was the day on which the early Danes used to go about begging for ale. Hence, it was the custom of the Island blacksmiths, after they had ceased firing, to conclude the day in public houses . . .' This seems a little contrived. St. Clement, Bishop of Rome, martyred by the Emperor Trajan, is more usually associated with a symbolic anchor. Tradition has it that he was tied to one and dropped into the sea.

A WIGHT CHRISTMAS

Down the centuries, Christmas celebrations on the Isle of Wight have generally mirrored those on the mainland. There have, however, been some distinctively local features.

In Yarmouth, for example, there was annually 'a thrill of excitement', according to local historian A.G. Cole, when the local butcher led round the streets a well-fatted ox from Thorley Farm which was to supply many of the onlookers with their Christmas dinner. Looking back on his nineteenth century childhood, Cole remembered how 'the butcher wore a spotlessly clean traditional blue serge apron and his captive ox would be carefully groomed and gaily adorned with holly and ribbons. As the little procession went along, it added a number of admirers and many halts were made when heads of families would come out of their homes and discussions took place on the savoury meat the ox would supply, and how the various cuts would be allocated. As a child, it always seemed to me extremely callous to mention these matters within hearing of the unfortunate animal.'

Throughout the Isle of Wight (as in England as a whole), an eagerly-anticipated Christmas tradition was the Mummers' play, performed annually by groups of costumed young men. The basic theme for all the many versions of this age-old Christmas pageant was the triumph of good over evil – but beyond that the plots and characters varied enormously across the country as the scripts (the term is used loosely since little was ever consigned to paper) were handed down from generation to generation. There were, however, some constants. 'Good' was always represented by Saint (or King) George and 'Bad', either by the traditional dragon or – in a throwback to the probable origins of the play at the time of the Crusades – by a fiendish Turkish knight. It is the Turk who tends to crop up the most in written references to mummers' performances on the Isle of Wight.

Writing in 1925, Ethel C. Hargrove described one local version of the play as featuring 'Father and Mother Christmas and their four sons, King George and Valiant Soldier (English), Noble Captain (French) and Keritick Knygth (Turkish)' and outlines the plot as follows: 'The Turk suggests making King George into a Christmas pie, and the enraged Sovereign knocks him down. Father Christmas weeps over his son's untimely end, but he is "patched up" by a surgeon. King George and the

Frenchman fight till the surgeon's aid is again required. In conclusion, Father and Mother Christmas come to blows.' Quite what Valiant's role was in this particular variation – which seems to have strayed somewhat from the original basic plot – is left unexplained by Hargrove, but he was evidently cast as a knight in a Yarmouth version described by A.G. Cole, alongside the inevitable Turkish foe, a bellman (town crier) 'and other legendary characters.'

Generally, the list of characters in the Island plays were much the same, but local variations meant that, for example, the popular character Little Johnny Jack appeared in some areas of the Island, but not in others. The Mummers' play was sometimes called *The Pageant of St. George* (among a host of optional titles), but on the Isle of Wight 'Christmas bwoys' usually served as sufficient description for this early form of knockabout entertainment. Happily, the complete dialogue of one of the local versions is preserved in W.H. Long's dictionary of the local dialect.

Family entertainment at Christmas was, of necessity, 'home-grown'. Local people had a wide choice of traditional games, some of which seem to have been specific to the Island. A particular favourite was Mariners, which apparently had at least three optional titles – Siege of Troy, Nine Men's Morris (a name which is actually mentioned by William Shakespeare) and Peg Nine Holes. It was played on a draughts board, if one was available, though improvisation was more usually the order of the day, with upturned wooden corn bins serving as the board or – if the weather permitted – a rough plan cut into the turf. Thought by some to date from the days of the Vikings, Mariners was played by two people, each equipped with nine pegs, or stones, which – since this was essentially a rustic form of chess – were known as pawns. Evidently, the local version of the game had its own characteristics. As recently as the 1920s, 'Isle of Wight Mariners' was found to be thriving in the USA!

A game involving considerably more than two people was known as the Farmer in his Den. Those taking part formed a ring with 'the farmer' standing in the middle. He selected a wife and the two, linking arms, danced round inside the ring. The wife then chose a child and the three of them danced and sang, then the child selected a nurse – and so it went on until a 'cheese' was picked from the remaining members of the ring. The cheese was not a good thing to be. He or she would have to submit to a ritual 'beating' by the whole of the assembled company. However, the cheese, once recovered, would quickly gain revenge with automatic selection for the farmer's role in the next round of the game.

Christmas church services clearly had something of a local flavour.

Newchurch historian Jack Lavers recalled a favourite carol regularly sung at the village's All Saints Church. Utilising the common Isle of Wight prefix 'wold', it was known as *The Wold Hark*.

Back at home, before the advent of mass-produced alternatives, Christmas decorations were provided by nature. While the holly bush was the most common source, a variety of evergreens were hung by country folk. They employed the ultimate economy of expression to describe them – all were simply known as 'Christmas'.

Prince Albert is credited with the introduction of the now-traditional
Christmas tree to England, and in this drawing by Dennis Burden is shown
with Queen Victoria and some of their children at Osborne House, where the
Christmas tree was very much a feature.

WASSAILING IN THE WIGHT

Usually defined in fairly general terms as merry-making, festive drinking and the like, wassailing has its origins in the Saxon toast *Waeshael*, meaning 'good health' or 'be healthy', and is tied to the yearly harvesting of apples. Ancient customs associated with wassailing were fairly common up until the nineteenth century, but are today observed by only a few communities in England. While all seemed to have been firmly linked to the Christmas and New Year period, the precise date for the ritual clearly varied. In some areas it was a Twelfth Night custom; in others, it was held on New Year's Eve. At Yarmouth on the Isle of Wight the children of the town annually went wassailing on New Year's Day.

The key feature of this ritual was the communal wassail bowl, usually made of ash or maple and filled with hot, spiced ale, roasted apples, eggs, cream and sugar (a concoction sometimes called 'lamb's wool'). While it was also customary to pass round a suitably decorated wassail bowl at private gatherings, the more usual way of observing the custom was to embark on a wassailing tour of the local neighbourhood, offering a drink from the bowl – sometimes in exchange for food.

In Yarmouth, as elsewhere (though possibly nowhere else on the Isle of Wight itself), the town's young 'wassailers' would annually carry a wassail cup, trimmed with ribbons and prominently displaying a large golden apple, from house to house. At each door they would announce their arrival with the local version of the traditional 'letting-in' song:

> Wassail, wassail to your town,
> The cup is white, and the ale is brown;
> The cup is made of the ashen tree,
> And the ale is brewed of good barley;
> Little maid, little maid, turn the pin,
> Open the door and let us in;
> God be here, and God be there,
> We wish you all a happy new year.

The associated Twelfth Night custom of wassailing the apple tree itself, a tradition of the cider-making regions in the South and West of England, was also observed on the Island. Contemporary reports in the *Isle of Wight County Press* confirm that it was an annual ritual on the Island well into the present century. After a meal in the farmhouse, the farmer would lead his workers into the orchard. Seizing a branch of an apple tree, he then recited the following:

> O apple tree, I wassail thee,
> In hopes that thou wilt blow
> To blow and bear well,
> So merry let us be;
> For the Lord doth know where we shall be
> To be merry another year.

Although this is the verse recorded in the newspaper, it is a considerably shortened version of the song traditionally associated with the custom. That is no surprise. Six lines of simple verse are easy to remember, Recalling the full text of the apple orchard song – especially after a slap-up Twelfth Night meal – would have been beyond most of the wassailers. The surviving remnants of the song, as performed on the Island, can be easily identified in the following 'un-cut' version:

> Old apple tree, we wassail thee,
> and hoping thou wilt bear.
> For the Lord doth know where we shall be,
> till apples come another year.
> To bear well and bloom well
> so merry let us be.
> Let every man take off his hat
> and shout to the old apple tree.
> Old apple tree, we wassail thee,
> and hoping thou wilt bear.
> Hat-fulls, cup-fulls, three-bushel bag-fulls,
> and a little heap under the stairs.
> Hip! Hip! Hooray!

On completion of the song, guns were fired through the branches of the apple tree – the original idea having been to scare away evil spirits. That done, it was customary for the health of the orchard to be toasted in warm cider, which usually contained pieces of toasted bread. This was passed round the assembled gathering in a rudimentary wassail bowl – normally a bucket! Some of the cider was then fed to the roots of a tree, while the remaining pieces of drink-sodden toast were left on the boughs, originally as a gesture of thanks to a guardian spirit.

A modern echo of the old traditions emerged in 1996 with the designation of 21 October as Apple Day – an attempt to raise awareness of the English apple. It was marked on the Island with appropriate events centred on commercial orchards at Freshwater and Gurnard.

GROWING PAINS

Snake's-stang, snake's-stang viee all about the brooks,
And sting all the bad bwoys that vor the fishes looks;
But let all the good bwoys ketch all the fish they can,
And car 'em away hooam to fry 'em in the pan.
Bren butter they sholl yet at supper wi' their fish,
But all the little bad bwoys sholl onny lick the dish.

For snake's-stang read dragon-fly – a less than welcome feature of the countryside among the young people of rural Wight in years gone by. Particularly large and vividly-coloured specimens frequented the Island, which may explain the unusual dread in which they were held by children. They were popularly supposed to possess a sting as venomous as the bite of an adder – hence the local name.

The dragon-fly was regarded as the guardian of the fish which lived in the brooks and ponds they frequented. The venomous sting the insect supposedly employed was an effective deterrent against those children who tried to catch the fish. There was, however, a qualification to this traditional scare story. The insect had no objection, apparently, to children who were normally well-behaved (the 'good bwoys') and was only a threat to those who weren't (the 'bad bwoys'). A useful parental ploy for ensuring the offspring did as they were told!

The young people themselves, were never quite sure whether they fitted the good category or the bad. On the appearance of the dreaded snake's stang, we learn from W.H. Long's nineteenth century guide to the Isle of Wight dialect, they would sing or chant the above rhyme 'as a kind of charm or protection against the noxious insect.' Interestingly, there are close equivalents to the local name for the dragon-fly in Northern dialects – 'horse's stang' and 'bull stang' were both used in Cumbria.

If the dragon-fly's venomous sting was imaginary, the sting of the 'sterrup' was anything but. Cobblers used the leather sterrup (stirrup) to hold a boot in place while it was being sewed. It was also frequently utilised for an altogether different purpose. Unsuspecting or dull youths (as Long describes them) were often sent by their seniors to the village cobbler with a request for 'sterrup ile'. The 'ile' (oil) they sought was never handed out in quite the manner expected. It consisted of a hearty whack across the shoulders with the sterrup!

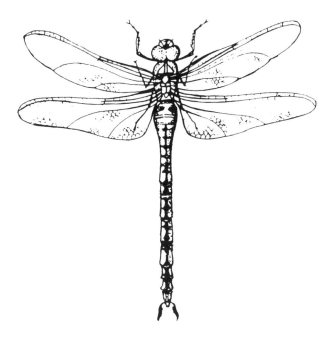

'Snake's stang' – the much feared Isle of Wight dragonfly.

Long's verbal illustration of this painful learning experience is a gem and well worth repeating in full: 'When I was a gurt hard bwoy, one time, out in the rickess at Wroxall wi' that 'ere maggoty Sam Jacobs, a zed to me: "Goo down to cobbler Coombes's vor me, wull'ee, and ax 'en to gee ye a drop o' hes best sterrup ile; there's noo call vor ye to take anything to car et in." Zo, like a fool, off I goos, and axed the wold man vor't. A was zet there, zowen away; but as zoon as I told'n what I was come vor, a razed up and took hes sterrup off his knee, and draaed en dree or vower times right across my shoulders, ready to cut me all to pieces. "There's the ile," a zays, "and I've rubbed it in vor thee". I roared out, and shabbed off as quick as I could, looken middlen foolish; and I've always minded what sterrup ile was vrom that day to this.'

Some translation is required in order to fully appreciate the above. The 'rickess' was the local name for a rickyard; 'maggoty' described someone who was unpredictable, acting on a whim; 'a' was commonly used instead of the pronoun 'he' on the Island; 'axed' was the dialect word for 'asked'; 'shabbed off' was the local way of saying 'sneaked out'; and 'middlen' meant 'exceedingly' in this instance, although, confusingly, the same word was also used at times for 'moderate'. Substitute 's' for 'z' in places; 'f' for 'v' in others and the charm of the story is revealed.

There were painful lessons, too, on reaching adulthood – especially out in the fields during the harvest. Anyone caught helping himself to more food than he could manage, drinking more than his allowance or committing any other offence against the rustic code was liable to be 'cobbed'. The beating that followed his being seized by his mates – the 'cob' – was usually administered with a boot. The unfortunate culprit could expect to receive six or twelve blows, depending on the gravity of his offence. It was all supposedly in fun!

Lessons in life were not, of course, always learnt the hard way. Isle of Wight children in the early nineteenth century received the first basics in numeracy much as their late twentieth century contemporaries do today – via their toes. A nursery jingle commonly used in counting the toes of infants has been recorded for posterity in local dialect. Substitute 'threshold' for the dialect word 'dreshel' and the rest is easy to follow:

> This gurt pig zays, 'I wants meeat';
> T'other one zays, 'Wher'll ye hay et?'
> This one zays, 'In granfer's barn';
> T'other one zays, 'I'll tell!'
> The little one zays, 'Week, Week!'
> I can't git over the dreshel.'

TRADITIONALLY TASTY TREATS

Among the tastier traditions of Wight is the doughnut. For the proof of the pudding, as it were, reference can be made to this book extract from 1861: 'Now, I fancy you are wondering what a doughnut can be; you can never have tasted one if this is your first visit here, for doughnuts are peculiar to the Isle of Wight, though I have heard they were originally derived from the Dutch and are to be met with in America.'

The passage is taken from *The Queen's Isle*, by A. Raine, who used not inconsiderable flair in describing what was clearly at the time an unfamiliar culinary delight.

'Well, then,' he wrote, 'picture yourself a round ball of dough, quite brown outside; now, open it – oh! there is a little cluster of plums in the middle. I remember – and it is one of the earliest things I do remember – when I was scarcely more than a baby, finding myself in a strange place, where they gave me toys to play with and "birds nests" to eat – so they called the several doughnuts then, to please me, the petted child; and years after, when I knew not I had ever seen the Isle of Wight, and all other kindnesses there had been forgotten, I was still haunted by the vague recollections of some place I had visited in early babyhood, where "birds nests" and playthings made so deep an impression on my infantine fancy.'

It is possible to find earlier written references to doughnuts on the Island. They crop up, for example, in some local versions of the shroving song and certainly seem to have been a culinary treat here far longer than on mainland England. Perhaps it was the international trade of the port of Cowes which was responsible for their early import into Wight. Whether or not the tradition of the Island being the 'birthplace' of the doughnut is true, there is no doubt that the lard-browned doughnuts of Wight have an impressive and distinctive pedigree.

The recipe for the true Isle of Wight doughnut never seems to have included jam. Plums may have been the early sweetener, but currants and candied peel were an optional – or perhaps replacement – filling. Local historian Johanna Jones has recalled that the Island's doughnut was smaller than the norm, about the size of a small orange, and that Westmore's Doughnut Shop, on the corner of Scarrots Lane and

Lower St. James Street, was the place to stock up on this noted delicacy.

Nothing like as delicate on the palette was Isle of Wight cheese. Made from skimmed milk, it became exceedingly dry and hard through keeping. This distinctive cheese rejoiced in the highly descriptive name of 'chockdog' (alternatively written as choke-dog) and was also known as Isle of Wight Rock! Its reputation has long survived its manufacture and the stories told of this extraordinary food are legion. Whether they are fact or legend is open to question.

Among the best of the chockdog tales relates how, during one of the frequent French raids on the Island, the local defenders ran short of lead. So they used their lunch instead, cutting up their cheese into bone-hard pellets, ramming these into the barrels of their guns and firing, apparently to great effect, upon the enemy.

In his 1866 dictionary of the local dialect, William Long tells of an Isle of Wight cheese being sent to someone 'at a distance' as a present. 'The recipient, not for a moment suspecting it was anything meant to be eaten, with great difficulty cut a hole through the middle of it, fitted it up and used it for a grindstone with success.' Happily, Long also included a memorable anecdote in local dialect about the 'delights' of bread and cheese (bren cheese) Isle of Wight style:

'Wold Jem Shotter over at Brison went one day on a arrant to Yafford, and when a was there Missus axed 'em if a would hay a bit o' bren cheese and a drop o' beer; but Jem zet and looked at it, and didn't offer to begin. "What's the matter, Jem?" zays Missus, "ye got what ye wants, han't ye?" "Noa, not quite, missus," zays Jem, "I wants the billhook to cut the cheese wi." Jem never got noo bren cheese there noo moore aater that.'

Islanders sometimes extended the use of the term 'chockdog' to describe tough pastry or hard food in general. Forest House Pudden, on the other hand, was very specific.

Forest House was the local name for the Isle of Wight's House of Industry (workhouse), established between 1770 and 1775 by gentlemen of the Island 'for the reception of the poor and ease of the poor rates.' It was among the first centralised workhouses in the country – individual parishes having until that time been responsible for taking care of their poor – and acquired the name Forest House owing to its nearness to Parkhurst Forest. The 'puddens' were a speciality of the place.

They were unappealingly made of flour, water and suet, without the saving graces of raisins, currants or sugar. It has been recorded that this dubious dish was served to the inmates of Forest House on Saturdays, though surviving workhouse menus from the mid-1830s show that, by then, a rather more appetising main meal – rice pudding with treacle – was the regular Saturday treat. The infamous flour and suet 'puddens' which had so singularly failed to raise the spirits are not mentioned.

They had, however, provided the ingredients for a well-aimed insult, as William Long recalled. In 1831, at the time of the nineteenth century democratic reform movement in England, what Long described as 'a tumultuous meeting' in favour of reform was held in the Corn Market at Newport. Farmers from Gatcombe village, vehemently opposed to the popular cause, were the butt of derisive cries from the crowd: 'Dree cheers vor the Forest House puddens!' they shouted. 'Why be we Forest House puddens?' asked one of the farmers in surprise. 'Because ye ha'nt got no raisins (reasons) in ye,' was the sharp-witted response.

ODDS AND ENDS:
A MISCELLANY

The people of the Isle of Wight have observed a number of other customs tied to the seasons, religious festivals and anniversaries in the annual calendar. Allied to the 'begging' customs of Shrove Tuesday were the activities of the 'Goodies' at Easter. These were old women who, starting early on Good Friday morning, went from door to door armed with large linen bags and asking for as much flour as the lady of the house could spare. The 'Goodies' later converted the contents of their, usually full, bags into fine white loaves for consumption on Easter Saturday.

Royal Oak (or Oakapple) Day on 29 May commemorated the 1651 concealment of Charles II in the famous Boscobel oak (although the date was actually the anniversary of his return to England after exile, when branches of the oak tree were displayed by monarchists). When, following the Restoration, it became established as an annual celebration, Royal Oak Day was closely allied to the traditional Maytime customs banned under the Puritans – who had even outlawed the maypole as an unacceptable fertility symbol! The emphasis on 29 May, however, was on the wearing of oak-leaf sprigs.

Country folk called the oak-sprigs chick-chacks (or shick-shacks). As elsewhere, 29 May was eventually known on the Island as Chick-Chack Day, and in local dialect . . .

The twenty-ninth of May is Zhick Zhack Day,
Zo mount your oak my bwoys an' gie a hip hooray!

Island children, especially the boys, continued to display the oak-sprigs – with an oakapple attached whenever possible – well into the present century, and the custom was extended in some places – Whippingham School is among those recorded – to a game of concealment. The oak-sprig was hidden in clothing or shoes, and children challenged each other to reveal its whereabouts with a version of the 29 May rhyme. Those who failed to produce a sprig were subjected to pinching, punching, pulling of hair . . . or more likely a combination of all three!

Whitsuntide festivals – or 'Whitsunales' – were once common on the

The mysterious Long Stone, the monolith after which the village of
Mottistone is named, has provoked both speculation and superstition
among Island folk down the ages.

Island. Local communities would choose two of their number as 'Lord and Lady of the Ale' and a large, empty building – usually a barn – was set aside as 'The Lord's Hall' for an evening of song and games. This was an ancient custom, dating back at least to the sixteenth century, when Whitwell's festival venue was the village 'churchhouse'.

Isle of Wight church weddings were often celebrated before Sunday morning service, and were followed by an immediate separation. This was back in the days of the divided congregation, when men and women sat apart from each other in church. Having 'tied the knot', the happy couple took up their seats for the morning service which followed the nuptials on opposite sides of the church! Reunited outside, many Island couples began married life seated in a brightly decorated farm waggon, hauled by a team of smartly turned-out horses, complete with dangling bells, which would take them to the marital home. 'Waggon weddings' died out with the advent of motorised transport, but did enjoy the occasional early twentieth century revival in Shorwell and other parts of rural Wight.

At funerals, sprigs of rosemary were handed round to mourners before the coffin left the house. Taken to the church, the sprigs were later ceremonially dipped into the grave as a mark of respect. Rosemary, along with spice, was also an ingredient of the cakes traditionally distributed at Isle of Wight funerals – though probably not at a burial which took place at Scratchells Bay, in the far west of the Island. Tradition asserts that, for fear his wife should dance over his grave – as she had threatened – a local man gave orders that his body should be submerged in the bay!

What sort of people were buried in the long barrow guarded over by the prehistoric Long Stone, above Mottistone, can only be guessed at. A visit to the famous monolith and its recumbent partner won't supply the answer, but may well reveal something about your own character. According to some local story-tellers, a child might easily swing the huge stone backwards and forwards, but a 'mighty man' with great strength would fail to move it – if he had 'guilt on his soul'.

The custom of 'ringing the curfew' was observed in Newport far longer than in most English towns. When introduced nationwide by William I as a key security measure, the evening eight o'clock bell signalled the start of a period during which the conquered English were forbidden to light fires or have any form of lighting in their home. Brading's municipal records show the curfew bell in nightly use there in the mid-sixteenth century – the curfew was lifted by a further ringing of the bell at 4am – but it was at Newport that the curfew bell was last heard on the Island. Though, by then, the bell simply 'tolled the knell of

Yarmouth's most famous seafarer was Sir Robert Holmes, commemorated by this statue in the town's church. Tradition suggests that while the head is undoubtedly that of the seventeenth century swashbuckler and Governor of the Isle of Wight, the body is actually that of Louis XIV. Holmes captured the statute and its sculptor from a French vessel and ordered the latter to remove the king's head and replace it with an image of Holmes himself. The result is a head rather too large for the body beneath!

the parting day,' the *Isle of Wight County Press* confirms its continuance at Newport into the latter years of the nineteenth century – with the morning bell at 6am in summer and an hour later in winter.

Perhaps the best-known tradition associated with bells on the Island is the couplet which tells how . . .

Shalfleet poor and simple people
Sold their bells to build a steeple.

As to when this actually happened, the guide produced for Shalfleet's Church of St. Michael the Archangel opts for around 1800 when the church's former wooden steeple – removed in 1912 – was built. Church archives seem to rule out earlier possibilities. The bells may have been sold with the church's three-pounder gun! Rhymes telling basically the same story exist elsewhere in the country.

CARICATURING THE CAULKHEADS

The Isle of Wight is a part of England. It also manages to remain distinctly and resolutely apart from it at the same time. And not just in a physical sense. Visitors from the mainland are only half-joking when they talk about 'going abroad' to the Isle of Wight. The ferry crossing from Portsmouth, Southampton or Lymington carries them to an enchanted offshore paradise where life is played out at a noticeably less frenetic pace. Where time sometimes appears to have stood still for centuries. And where, of course, the local people still go around on all fours.

Of all the many scandalous stories told in the mother country about the people of offshore Wight, the tradition that they have yet to master the technique of walking upright has perhaps been the most often repeated. In fact, this mocking observation is actually enshrined in local folklore, which insists that the original inhabitants of the isle did, indeed, move about on their hands and knees. When a visitor from England suggested an upright position might be preferable, the local folk, holding up their hands, replied: 'Then what shall us do with these?' Having considered the dilemma for a while, they came up with the answer themselves – and put their hands in their pockets. 'Where, of course,' concludes the tale, 'they have remained ever since.' Parsimony is another of the supposed characteristics which traditionally set the people of Wight apart from the rest!

Indolence is yet another. Everyone living on the Island was at one time reputed to be lazy by nature. That's a whole lot of 'lerrups' – the Islanders' own dialect word for lazy, slovenly fellows. The term 'Isle of Wight Dog' had no canine associations – it was commonly and specifically used at one time to describe a fit of laziness. And laziness, it is true, seems to have developed into something of an art form among certain sections of the Island community, though those who practiced it laid the blame fully on an imaginary being called 'Larrance'. His very name was a widely-used pseudonym for indolence – and his influence was strong. 'I can't git up, mayet, vor Larrance got hold on me,' is recorded by most of the local dialect experts as the typical response of a sluggish labourer.

Jack Lavers' most recently published dictionary of Isle of Wight words recalls the Lazy Club, membership of which seems to have been barred to all but the most indolent of the local population. 'At Arreton, in the early years of the century,' he records, 'it was said that one villager was thrown out of the Lazy Club – he was seen kneeling down to pull rhubarb when he could have been laid down.'

Retreating further into history, we find that slinging insults at the people of Wight was customary in the sixteenth century. An indignant Sir John Oglander, the noted Island diarist, records the most common reproach of the time: 'It is, and hath bene a tax layd on this island, that it never produced any extraordinary fayr handsome woman, nor a man of any supereminent gifts in witt or wisdome, or a horse excellent for goodness. I can answer, that no part of England in generall, the quantitie considered, hath produced more exquisite in eyther species than this island.'

The accusation that Island men lacked 'witt or wisdome' was a common slur. Compilers of British folk tales list more than 40 specific locations in the British Isles supposedly inhabited by simpletons. Three larger areas are also included: the Lincolnshire Fens, Sutherland in Scotland – and the whole of the Isle of Wight.

While Islanders may themselves have contributed to some of the many unflattering stories told about their collective character and appearance, most are, of course the work of mischief-making 'knownuthen' mainlanders. The people of Wight have a single word for their neighbours on the mainland which, while it may not be spat out today with quite the same degree of contempt as in centuries past, still has the capacity to convey an element of hostility towards the folk from over the water.

The work 'overner' seems to have developed as a short form of 'overrun feller.' While it can – and often is – applied to anyone who is not a native of the Isle of Wight, it is more specifically reserved for mainland 'immigrants'. No matter how long you may have lived on the Island, you're destined to remain an overner unless you can prove you were born there. The term is unquestionably much older than that commonly used to distinguish Islanders from the rest of humankind – 'caulkheads' – which is derived from the act of caulking (waterproofing) the hulls of ships. Actually, the traditional name for a native of Wight is Vectensian, derived from Vectis – the Roman name for the Island. Caulkhead (sometimes 'corkhead') seems to have been invented in Southampton to describe those Islanders who, short of work at home, crossed the Solent to caulk vessels in the city's shipyards.

The following extract, courtesy of William Long, needs no further comment (other than to explain that a 'Luccomer' was the local name in the east of the Island for a storm blowing up from the south-east – the direction of Luccombe village – and 'vokes,' as may be guessed, was the local way of saying 'folks' or people):

'Had a miserable rough night, you.'

'Oi, you, 'twas a regular Luccomer last night.'

'I wish it had capsized they there overners, comen across; what do they want over here, tryen to take the bread out o' vokes mouths?'

Hospitable people though the caulkheads undoubtedly are, they retain a strong and distinctive insular identity which the resident overners in their midst ignore at their peril – especially when they try to teach them how to walk on two legs!

FURTHER READING

Adams, W.H. Davenport, *The History, Topography and Antiquities of the Isle of Wight* (London), 1856

Albin, J., *A New, Correct & Much Improved History of the Isle of Wight* (Newport, Isle of Wight), 1795

Atkins, R.J., (article) *Islander Magazine* (Seaview, Isle of Wight), 1975

Barber, Thomas, *Picturesque Illustration of the Isle of Wight* (London), 1831

Bartlett, W.H., *Niton, Isle of Wight: Its Undercliff & Neighbourhood* (Newport, Isle of Wight), 1928

Boase, Wendy, *The Folklore of Hampshire and the Isle of Wight* (London), 1976

Bord, Janet & Colin, *Earth Rites* (London), 1982

Bord, Janet & Colin, *Sacred Waters: Holy Wells and Water Lore in Britain and Ireland* (London), 1985

Briggs, Katharine, *A Dictionary of British Folk Tales*, Parts A & B (London), 1970/71

Cole, A.G., *Yarmouth Isle of Wight* (Newport, Isle of Wight), 1948

Coleman, S.Jackson (edit), *Vectigalia: Local Legends in Britain's Garden Isle* (London), 1950

Davenport Adams, W.H., *The History, Topography and Antiquities of the Isle of Wight* (London and Ryde, Isle of Wight), 1856

Dowling, John, *Fifty Fascinating Facts about the Isle of Wight* (Ventnor, Isle of Wight), 1984

Du Boulay, E., *Bembridge Past and Present* (Ryde, Isle of Wight), 1911

Dyer, Barbara, *St. Helens Sports & Carnival – A History* (St. Helens, Isle of Wight), 1991

Eldridge, R.J., *Newport Isle of Wight in Bygone Days* (Newport, Isle of Wight), 1952

Evans, The Rev. James, *The Legend of Lucy Lightfoot* (Gatcombe, Isle of Wight), 1960

Frazer, Oliver, *The Natural History of the Isle of Wight* (Wimborne, Dorset), 1990

Frost, Richard, *Isle of Wight Mysteries* (Shanklin, Isle of Wight), 1980

Fry, A.W., *The History of God's Providence House* (Newport, Isle of Wight), 1939; revised 1966

Hallam, Dr. Elizabeth (edit), *The Plantagenet Chronicles* (London), 1986

Hargrove, Ethel C., *England's Garden Island* (Newport, Isle of Wight), 1926

Hockey, S.F., *Insula Vecta* (Chichester, Sussex), 1982

Jones, Jack & Johanna, *The Isle of Wight: An Illustrated History* (Wimborne, Dorset), 1987

Knighton, Charles, *The Customs and Ceremonies of Britain: An Encyclopaedia of Living Traditions* (London), 1986

Lavers, Jack, *The Dictionary of Isle of Wight Dialect* (Wimborne, Dorset), 1988

Long, W.H., *A Dictionary of the Isle of Wight Dialect* (Newport, Isle of Wight), 1886

Mills, A.D., *The Place-Names of the Isle of Wight* (Stamford, Lincolnshire), 1996

Noyes, Hugh (edit), *The Isle of Wight Bedside Anthology* (Bognor Regis, Sussex), 1951

Oglander, Sir John (Edit. W.H. Long), *The Oglander Memoirs* (London), 1888

Roach Smith, C. & Smith, H., *Original Glossaries – Isle of Wight Words* (London), 1881

Searle, Adrian, *A Century of Carnival* (Ryde, Isle of Wight), 1988

Shepard, Bill, *Newport Isle of Wight Remembered* (Newport, Isle of Wight), 1984

Sheridan, W.C.F.G., *A Topographical and Historical Guide to the Isle of Wight* (London), 1833

Stone, P.G., *The Architectural Antiquities of the Isle of Wight* (London), 1891

Stone, P.G., *Legends and Lays of the Isle of Wight* (London), 1912

Turner, Edward (edit), *Encyclopaedia of Isle of Wight Words, Place-Names, Legends, Books and Authors*, 1900

Venables, Canon Edmund, *The Isle of Wight* (Stanford), 1860

Whitehead, Dr. John L., *The Undercliff of the Isle of Wight* (London),1911

Worsley, Sir Richard, *History of the Isle of Wight* (London) 1781

Newspapers – various articles:
Isle of Wight County Press
Isle of Wight Observer

ACKNOWLEDGEMENTS

Many people have given their time and expertise during the preparation of this book. I extend my thanks to all who have contributed.

Some deserve special mention: Ryde historian, Roy Brinton, for allowing me access to his extensive local history and picture archives; Diane Coppell for proof-reading the early drafts; and Marie Rankin for her help with specific research matters. Thanks also go to my publisher, David Burnett (The Dovecote Press), for his support and enthusiasm.

The majority of the illustrations were specially drawn for this book by Dennis Burden from photographs taken by Patrick Eden. Their joint contribution – which has so enhanced this finished product – was invaluable.

Other illustrations were either from the author's own collection or from the following specific sources: R. E. Brinton Collection for the illustration from the Isle of Wight Pageant (page 85) and the original photographs from which Dennis Burden made his drawings of Brading Bull Ring (page 90) and the Hare and Hounds pub (page 98); National Maritime Museum/Greenwhich Hospital Collection for the portrait of Admiral Hopsonn (page 77); The British Museum for the portrait of George Morland (page 81); Ventnor and District Local History Society for the illustration by Joan Gordon of Newport's 'Bargan Zatterdays' (page 105); Hutchinson & Co., publishers, for the drawing of the pancake race (page 111) from *British Folk Customs*, by Christina Hole, 1976.